CONTENTS

Part Three – Finding Your Inspiration

ACKNOWLEDGMENTS

I would like to express my heartfelt gratitude to my beloved wife Melissa, as well as our three precious children, Gifford, Jania, and Jaydon. Their unyielding support has been an immense source of strength for me and has helped me navigate through life's challenges with greater ease. I am truly blessed to have such a wonderful family who always has my back.

My humble appreciation goes out to my 5.3+M Leadership First family. Your steadfast backing and unwavering support have been instrumental in bringing this book to fruition, and for that, I am forever grateful. Without your remarkable encouragement, this project would not have seen the light of day. Thank you all from the bottom of my heart.

INTRODUCTION

For 20 years, John sat in his chair, struggling to find meaning and purpose in his job. Sadly, the company work environment became toxic to the core resulting in new employees quitting within six months of joining, and the people who gave their blood, sweat and tears to the organization felt uncertain, uninspired, and unenthusiastic about their work and the company's future.

John felt dejected and unmotivated. He eventually left the company to follow his heart to pursue something that provided some sense of fulfillment for his life but, more importantly, to add value to the people he was entrusted to serve. This story is so familiar, organizations with no purpose, no vision, no values, and absolutely no communication holding on by a shoestring of existence quite comfortable with being average instead of being extraordinary.

An organization with these tendencies suffers from a lack of inspired leadership. Unfortunately, these leaders are so blinded by their limitations;

they block any attempt by anyone to remove the silos and status quo that allow their team to become inspired and excited about their work. Time and time again, history has proven that leadership makes a huge difference in any company. A leader can walk into a room of depressed, uninspired people and transform that environment into one of hope, inspiration, motivation, belief, vision and purpose; that's the power of an inspirational leader. For instance, a new plant manager looking for ways to control costs decided to change the company's culture. The plant manager challenged his team to deliver a complex equipment upgrade project on time and on budget, which was at significant risk of failing on both counts.

His team, however, miscalculated and over-ordered stainless-steel pipes and fittings for the job. However, still operating within the basic assumptions of the long-standing culture, they hid their mistake, fearful of being criticized and punished. Before starting the project, the manager told his team they must let go of their fears and find new ways of working together. This was a powerful reminder of how strong a grip the basic assumptions can have on thinking and behavior: Despite a consistent message from the new plant manager that everyone is safe to voice their concerns and suggestions without any form of punishment and discrimination, the past was still very much alive for this team.

Finally, recognizing they could not deliver on their commitments without correcting their mistake and aligning their behavior with two of the espoused station values, transparency and learning from mistakes, the team took the needed steps to return the materials and salvage the budget. As a result, the power plant made great strides under the new manager and built a more positive and productive culture during his one-year period. As a result of his leadership, the plant manager began to see that his focus on communicating a vision and setting challenges was shifting employee behavior, strengthening morale, and improving performance. As a matter of fact, performance improved significantly with essentially the same workforce, the same external environment, and the same leadership team. Early signs showed that a culture of collaboration and teamwork replaced the long-standing culture of fear and mistrust. Every leader who seeks to make deep-seated changes that challenge the status quo will come up against significant challenges that seek to limit and, in many instances, stand in the way of any change. In the face of resistance and the inevitable slow pace of change, it's natural, but unproductive, to fall back on old patterns. If this happens, a leader risks reinforcing the culture they are trying to change, which will be detrimental to the whole process.

For the plant manager, returning to old behaviors of showing frustration and impatience, publicly scolding and criticizing people, and making unilateral decisions would only confirm for everyone what they still truly believed – that nothing would change. It took a consistent effort to look inward to ensure he acted as a more consistent role model. It takes absolutely nothing to continue with the status quo and settle for "what is," but great leaders know that any meaningful change starts with a commitment from the leader, which then translates to the rest of the team.

As the leader, the buck stops with you; you have to take responsibility for the state of your company and the morale of your employees. So many organizations suffer from people sitting in leadership positions who have no business being there. These two stories are so real, one organization with no sense of leadership and the other showing what can happen to any company when someone has the mind of a leader and models the behavior they expect from their team. When you are a leader, you have the influence to lead people to greatness or lead them to despair. This book will help you find the inspiration within so you can plant seeds of hope in the hearts of your team, lead a change successfully and, most notably, awaken a sense of expectation inside of you and the people you lead. Nothing is more gratifying than providing hope to people from a struggling business, leading a turnaround, generating a profit and witnessing a profound change in people at your company. There's a reason why great organizations continue to dominate their industry and frustrate their competition because they are grounded in inspirational leadership.

These organizations understand that with the proper foundation in place, with inspirational leadership at every nook and cranny within the company, these organizations achieve some of the most incredible feats in business, lifting the company to an extraordinary level that adds tremendous value to the people they are entrusted to serve. What makes you effective as a leader is not the title you hold. Instead, it's demonstrating an unrelenting focus on helping others succeed in their collective efforts. Leadership has precious little to do with authority, management acumen, or even being in charge. Instead, leadership is all about people inspiring people to believe that the impossible is possible, developing and building confidence in people to perform at heights they never imagine.

Your position on the org chart doesn't make you a leader. Your title doesn't make you a leader. Leadership has nothing to do with your social status, your bank account, or where you reside. It's all about one life inspiring and motivating another to become the very best version of themselves. Each chapter in this book will help you find the inspiration within to become the leader you were destined to develop into. As John Quincy Adams puts it, "if your actions inspire others to dream more, learn more, do more and become more, you are a leader."

PART ONE

WHAT GREAT LEADERS DO

1

WHY GREAT LEADERS ARE GREAT LEARNERS

"Leaders Never Stop Learning"
Christine Cane

Imagine this for a second; In 1996, a web campaign was launched urging Apple enthusiasts to buy shares of the company to prove to Wall Street that Apple was still a relevant player in the industry. After Steve Jobs returned, Apple's fortunes significantly improved - an understatement, to say the least. In fact, it's worth noting that in 1997, Apple was teetering on the brink of bankruptcy until Microsoft and Bill Gates came to the rescue with a $150 million investment that helped set the company back on track.

Ryan Faas wrote in his article 'If you had told me years ago when I was reporting on Apple's change in leadership that the company would eventually have a market cap that topped Exxon Mobil's, making it one of the most valuable companies in the U.S. I'd have called you crazy." But it happened, and it took place under Steve Jobs' leadership. So what changed at Apple when Steve Jobs returned? First, Jobs made Apple's culture more agile, giving it a degree of flexibility comparable to that of a start-up. Apple's remarkable success as an innovative industry leader is primarily due to their exceptional flexibility and agility. Jobs also killed 70% of Apple's product line to give the company that degree of focus because they strayed too far from its core mission of offering personal computers. This strategic move allowed the company to concentrate its efforts on producing high-quality and innovative computer technology, ultimately leading to their success in the industry. Apple have consistently demonstrated an impressive ability to rapidly adapt to changes in technology and markets, resulting in the creation of groundbreaking products that have profoundly impacted the world.

This remarkable feat is attributed to the establishment of a culture of continuous learning and innovation, which has led to the disruption of many industries. Even in the face of Apple's success, Steve Jobs' unwavering commitment to learning and innovation serves as a powerful reminder that great leaders must never cease to learn. Life itself is one long learning experience, and the modern business world is evolving and changing at a breakneck pace. If your leadership has plateaued and you have no desire to learn anything new, it's time to do some soul-searching to figure out why. The leaders who do the most significant harm to an organization are the ones who think they have arrived; they stop growing, innovating and improving.

However, an organization will only grow when their leaders grow, which is why great leaders prioritize continuous learning and development for themselves and their teams. As a result, increasing your leadership ability also increases the overall success of your company and, in the process, continually adds value to the people you are privileged to lead. It's almost certain that leaders who engulf themselves in self-development lead companies that become one of the best in the world.

The Neuroplasticity Of Learning.

When you're learning, significant changes occur in your brain, including creating new connections between neurons. This phenomenon is called neuroplasticity. The more you practice, the stronger these connections become; as they strengthen, the messages are transmitted faster, making them more efficient. This is how you become better at anything you learn, whether it's playing football, reading, drawing, etc. We can compare the connections between your neurons to trails in a forest. Walking through a forest without a trail is difficult because you have to compact and push the vegetation and branches out of the way to carve your way through. But the more you use the same trail, the easier and more practicable it becomes. Conversely, when you stop using the trail, the vegetation grows back, and the trail slowly disappears.

This is very similar to what happens in your brain; when you stop practicing something, the connections between your neurons weaken and can ultimately be dismantled or pruned. That is why it is so difficult to start reading again when school begins if you have not read all summer. However, it is possible for some neural networks to become so strong that the trails or connections never completely disappear. As we learn, our brain literally remodels itself based on our new experiences.

When you change your beliefs and learn something new, you actually alter your brain's neurochemistry and structure. This is why LEADERS never stop learning. They challenge themselves to new levels of performance because if leaders aren't challenging themselves to do new things or take new risks, their own performance will be stagnated, which very often reflects back on those they lead. New levels of performance are achieved by doing things never done before.

Successful leaders keep their minds open to new things because there's always more to discover, no matter how high their level of mastery. Learning is the key to growth, and leaders who understand the purpose of continuous development raise the tide of everyone around them. According to Eric Hoffer: "In a time of drastic change, it is the learners who inherit the future. The learned usually find themselves equipped to live in a world that no longer exists." Suppose you're the kind of leader who finally becomes a CEO or whatever your dream job is and you stop craving knowledge, according to Alyssa Satara.

In that case, you'll hinder your ability to lead. Great leaders prioritize learning because they prioritize growing. Learn your market, learn about your employees, and learn about different industries because these variables are continuously changing. If you want to be an incredible leader in your industry, learning is where you should start.

Innovate or Die; How Your Brand Of Leadership Can Cripple Your Company.

Many people hold onto tradition because that's all they know but iconic leaders the world over challenged the status quo at some point because they understand that times are changing, and at some point, they will also have to change as well. So, ask yourself this question.

•What will be your leadership legacy when you depart from your company or when you depart from this planet?

•How will you be remembered as a leader?

Have you ever thought about it? Will you be classified as the leader who didn't take self-development seriously and didn't embrace the future but kept holding on to old practices by refusing to innovate your thinking and, by extension, your business? If Steve Jobs and Steve Wozniak did not challenge the idea of making a personal computer for everyone, there probably would not be an Apple today. Companies that strive for innovative thinking or innovative leadership are the ones that take a proactive approach to reconstructing and disrupting the markets by creating blue ocean opportunities for themselves. They don't just survive but thrive in tough times. As a result, the workplace becomes an exciting one full of creativity and imagination. Surprisingly, many organizations view innovation and continuous development as an option with little or no interest in either. This is rather alarming because innovation is no longer a luxury or an "accessory" but a necessity. The companies that totally neglected the warning signs of change played a huge price for it.

Let's look at a few examples:

Kodak

A generation ago, a "Kodak moment" meant something that was worth saving and savoring. Given that Kodak's core business was selling film, it is not hard to see why the last few decades proved challenging. According to Scott Anthony, a contributor for the Harvard Business Review, cameras went digital and then disappeared into cell phones. People went from printing pictures to sharing them online.

Kodak actually had most of the patents for the digital-photography technology, but it didn't commercialize them aggressively because that would have cannibalized its film business. Kodak was so blinded by its success that it completely missed the rise of digital technologies. Instead, other firms licensed Kodak's technology and commercialized it. But, unfortunately, Kodak couldn't make that switch from a culture of film to a culture of digital technology. So the company filed for bankruptcy protection in 2012, exited legacy businesses and sold off its patents before re-emerging as a sharply smaller company in 2013. Once one of the most influential companies in the world, today, the company has a market capitalization of less than $500 million.

Blackberry

BlackBerry devices were top in their class for many years because they provided small Qwerty keyboards that made it easier to fire off emails and instant messages. However, Apple and Android smartphone users became comfortable with touchscreen devices and actually preferred them for the larger screens. BlackBerry failed to innovate, and the company stuck doggedly to the idea that fiddly plastic keys were not only desirable but preferable to sleek, elegant devices and that if they churned out enough, they would still sell.

This never happened. The company did try to turn the corner with BlackBerry 10, which allowed it to create full touchscreen devices with a more modern look and feel, but by then, it was too late. BlackBerry has stopped designing its own phone and pivoted to become a cybersecurity firm, conversely bringing to an end one of the most iconic products of the internet era.

BlockBuster

Netflix's toppling of the traditional video-rental market, and especially the Blockbuster chain, will likely be studied by business students for years to come. Blockbuster CEO John Antioco was approached in 2000 by Netflix CEO and co-founder Reed Hastings about forming a partnership. According to Netflix CFO Barry McCarthy, "Reed had the audacity to propose to them that we run their brand online and that they run [our] brand in the stores, and they just about laughed us out of their office. At that point, Netflix had just tweaked the business model and had begun selling subscriptions in September 1999. "It was Reed's insight that the subscription model would resonate with consumers in a compelling way," McCarthy said. "He re-engineered the website and software to support a subscription model...we began to grow exponentially overnight. In 1998, I think the business did $1 million in revenue. In 1999, we did $5 million, then $35 million and then $75 million and $150 million and then almost $300 million...We were I think five years to $500 million and another three years to a $1 billion, all because of the subscription model." Now, Netflix has a market cap of $196.45 billion and is considered one of the world's most innovative companies; in 2010, Blockbuster filed for bankruptcy protection.

MySpace

From 2005 to 2008, MySpace reigned supreme. MySpace was the most visited social networking site in the world, even surpassing Google in June of 2006 as the most visited website in the United States. In addition, in 2005, MySpace CEO Chris DeWolfe met with Facebook co-founder Mark Zuckerberg and the pair talked merger.

Eventually, Mark asked Chris if MySpace wanted to buy Facebook for $75 million. Chris said no. When they met again later that year, Zuckerberg raised the price to $750 million, and DeWolfe again said no. Given the slow pace of innovation at MySpace since News Corp acquired them, it's entirely possible Facebook would never have become the cultural touchstone it is today under Chris and Tom's leadership instead of Mark's. Facebook has now exceeded $700 billion in market value, and Myspace is more of a Pandora Radio than a Facebook.

The world is very dynamic, and if your leadership is stagnant, especially with the pace of change in our world today, your organization will be rendered irrelevant. The more we learn, the more we grow, and the more we grow, the better we can serve others, our communities and the world. So make it a priority to learn and grow continuously; this will help you develop into a great leader.

2

HUMILITY IS THE ESSENCE OF GREAT LEADERSHIP

"Being humble means recognizing we are not on earth to see how important we can become, but to see how much difference we can make in the lives of others."
Gordon B. Hinckley

After completing law school, Darwin Smith joined Kimberly-Clark's legal department with the intention of gaining corporate law experience for a few years before starting his own firm. However, his plans took an unexpected turn. Darwin Smith was not only a long-term employee at Kimberly-Clark, but he also rose to the position of CEO. During his tenure, he successfully turned the company's fortunes around to the point where the success of Kimberly-Clark surpassed that of companies like Coke and 3M.

But what made Darwin Smith an outstanding leader was not his pictures on the cover of magazines or the God-like status given to many successful leaders. No, it was his humility and ability to stay true to his core values despite all his success. It has been proven through various research studies that leaders who possess humility are highly effective in inspiring teamwork, motivating their employees and achieving organizational goals. Although humility may not be the most obvious trait we associate with great business leaders, it is undoubtedly critical to their success. According to Jeff Hyman, what makes humility such an important quality? Humble leaders understand that they are not the smartest person in every room. Nor do they need to be. They encourage people to speak up, respect differences of opinion, and champion the best ideas, regardless of whether they originate from a top executive or a production-line employee.

When a leader harnesses input from everyone, it carries through the organization. As other executives and line managers emulate the leader's approach, a culture of getting the best from every team and every individual takes root. In short, leaders know how to get the most from people. When things go wrong, humble leaders admit to their mistakes and take responsibility. When things go right, they shine the spotlight on others.

At the heart of humility is a desire to serve and a dedication to helping others become great. That's the essence of leadership; helping your people reach their full potential, helping your team maximize their gifts, and helping people to become the best version of themselves. As mentioned above, the research is absolutely clear; positive, inspiring, and empowering leaders always become great leaders. They are valued more by their team, and they create great performing teams as a result. How can you incorporate humility into your leadership? Consider the following because employees who work under great leaders tend to be happier, more productive, and more connected to their organization – which has a ripple effect that reaches your business's bottom line.

Lead By Example

To effectively lead a team, one must always keep in mind the importance of setting a positive and constructive example. This duty extends to all scenarios, whether big or small and requires consistent effort and attention to detail. By modeling the behaviors and values that you wish to see in your team, you can inspire and motivate them to reach their full potential and achieve success together. Remember, as a leader, your actions speak louder than words, and your team will look to you for guidance and support in all aspects of their work.

Encourage Others To Grow

Humble leaders know that in today's fast-paced and competitive business environment, it is imperative for all employees to possess leadership skills. This facilitates swift decision-making and boosts customer satisfaction while saving valuable time, energy, and financial resources. Furthermore, delegating leadership responsibilities to capable employees can significantly reduce your workload and foster a positive work culture. By doing so, you can also minimize negative office gossip, increase employee engagement and productivity, resulting in a more efficient and effective workforce.

Have A Strong Vision

Humble leaders are very often great visionaries. Such leaders have a remarkable capacity to trust their instincts, think beyond the present, and imagine things that do not yet exist. Their unique perspective sets them apart from others and enables them to communicate their vision to their team effectively. They pursue their vision with unwavering determination until it becomes a reality.

Keep Developing Yourself

Humble leaders are those who are always willing to embrace new and innovative ideas. They understand that there is always room for growth and improvement, no matter how experienced they may be in their field. As emphasized in chapter one, continual learning and development are essential components of professional advancement. Leaders who prioritize ongoing education and skill-building are better equipped to lead their teams to new levels of success and achievement that were once thought impossible. By remaining open to new ideas and approaches, these leaders are able to inspire their teams and create a culture of growth and progress within their organizations.

Learn From Your Mistakes

Humble leaders take responsibility for EVERYTHING. They turn each misstep into an opportunity to learn instead of pointing fingers, according to Ron Gibori. They pull their thumb and ask themselves, "What could I have done differently?" They find a lesson, while others only see a problem. They privately address mistakes from their team but take the blame publicly without dissent. If someone slips up, they pick them up; they don't point fingers and pass the blame. When you lead a group of people, they become reflections of yourself, and when you are humble enough to admit your mistakes, it reinforces the habit of others to do the same.

Find Your Passion

Individuals exhibiting humble leadership qualities exude an unwavering commitment to their work that transcends self-imposed limitations. When working alongside such individuals, their contagious passion and infectious enthusiasm can inspire those around them to believe that they are capable of achieving anything they set their minds to. Collaborating with humble leaders can be a truly uplifting experience, as their unwavering dedication to their craft is both admirable and inspiring.

Keep A Positive Attitude

In difficult times, when things seem to be falling apart, and challenges arise, humble leaders motivate themselves with the mantra "I'm Going To

Make It" - no matter how hard it may seem. By cultivating a positive attitude, leaders create a ripple effect that inspires others to do the same within the organization.

Become Inspirational

Leaders who inspire their employees create high levels of engagement. This quality sets apart the best leaders from others, and it is what employees desire most in their leaders. A company with inspiring leaders at all levels of the organization has immense power. Such companies can achieve innovative and heroic accomplishments in business because their employees are motivated and inspired to make them happen.

Empathy

Leadership is all about people and relationships. Whether you're the leader of a small team, the manager of a large retail store, or the CEO of a global corporation, your people make your organization successful. Empathy is a vital part of emotional intelligence that humble leaders embrace. By recognizing and acknowledging the emotions of others, leaders can better understand their perspectives and build stronger relationships. Moreover, displaying these character traits can foster a more positive and inclusive work environment where all team members feel valued and supported. Therefore, it is crucial for leaders to cultivate these skills in order to create a cohesive and productive team.

It's important never to confuse humility with weakness; as a matter of fact, putting the needs of others before your own requires strong will and character. It also takes vulnerability and transparency to admit mistakes and show fallibility in front of your team. Humble leaders exhibit behaviors that lift their team's spirits, self-esteem, and confidence to achieve anything imaginable. Always remember how you treat people says a lot about you, and your leadership will be judged on how you inspire, influence, and motivate your people. It has nothing to do with how much money you have or your position or title; it has nothing to do with that. It's all about inspiring people to believe they can achieve anything beyond their own limiting beliefs.

Darwin Smith proves that humble leaders can achieve the unimaginable. Still, it all starts with a focus on the people you are entrusted to serve and your ability to drive people forward with excitement, inspiration, trust, and vision. Becoming one of the great leaders takes the strength of character and a firm commitment to do the right thing, at the right time, for the right reason. This means doing what you say when you say it and creating an environment of trust that allows everyone to produce their very best work.

3

CRITICAL HEALTH RELATED ISSUES FROM WORKING IN A TOXIC WORK ENVIRONMENT

"Nothing will kill a great employee faster than watching you tolerate a bad one"
- Perry Belcher.

"After working in a toxic environment for seven years, I decided to quit my job in a last-ditch attempt to save my sanity. After I quit, I went to the doctor who said my stress levels were dangerously high, and I was going to cause myself long term physical and mental health damage. I needed three months to recover from the trauma before I could face going back to work. I am still in the same profession now, but I choose to work for companies that take better care of their employees, and now I work much better hours, don't allow anyone to make me feel pressured, and I am open with my colleagues if I am struggling to cope. Now I put myself first, and I am no longer a people pleaser."

After reading this story from Faye Ekong's article, Surviving and Thriving A Toxic Workplace, I told myself this must be fictional; this can't be real. But after reading more stories like this, it is becoming a serious cause of concern because now you are talking about someone's health, and no job should ever be the cause of anyone's health-related issues. Nevertheless, the link between adverse health and a lousy workplace is "significant, profound, and has been documented over decades," according to Jeffrey Pfeffer, a professor of Organizational Behavior at Stanford Graduate School of Business and the author of "Dying for a Paycheck: How Modern Management Harms Employee Health and Company Performance and What We Can Do About It."

Pfeffer said it's a significant health crisis, resulting in over 120,000 excess deaths yearly in the United States. Yet, ironically, research shows that stressful workplaces aren't even good for employers. Pfeffer notes that stressed people are more likely to quit and come to work sick. And beyond a certain point, long work hours actually harm productivity. Pfeffer further argued that being in an awful job doesn't just impact your health directly. "People who are stressed are more likely to smoke more, drink more, they're more likely to overeat ... they're more likely to engage in illicit drug-taking, and they're less likely to exercise. So, stress affects not only people's health directly, but through its effect on their individual health-relevant behaviors." As indicated by Raven Ishak, here are some health-related issues from working in a toxic work environment you must be aware of and how they can negatively impact your health.

Depression

Working in an environment where a boss or co-worker mutes your talents and self-worth can amplify existing mental health issues which can lead to depression. Unfortunately, this toxic health issue doesn't just stay within the confines of your office. Depression can often leak into your personal life, making you second-guess yourself and your potential.

Insomnia

Falling and staying asleep might not be very high on your to-do list when you're expected to work around the clock. However, a toxic work environment can lead you to experience anxious thoughts at night, preventing you from getting enough quality shut-eye. But be careful of this becoming a lasting pattern, as your sleepless nights can impact your judgment, clarity, and perspective, preventing you from tackling future stressful situations.

Stress

While it would be a dream to refrain from stressing out at work, unfortunately, it comes with the paycheck. However, if your job doesn't give you a sense of purpose, you may want to reconsider your position. Jan Bruce, CEO and co-founder of meQuilibrium, told Fortune, "The data we collect while working with large communications, technology, and healthcare companies show among highly stressed employees, 72% report having a low connection to their work." This comes as no surprise when you look at the big picture. When there's a disconnection from the company's mission, the long hours and toxic bosses can cause you to stress out.

Fatigue.

Even when we say that we're going to stop working, we don't. This can make us feel fatigued and burnout. And while we could point the finger at ourselves, our company's toxic culture is also to blame. For instance, if your boss is sending you an email at 11 p.m., they're showing you that boundaries do not matter at your job. Pfeiffer explained to Slate Magazine that with technology, our employers are expecting us always to be "on." Even though this expectation might be true, it doesn't mean we should.

Anxiety.

Not only is a toxic work environment stressful, but it can also cause anxiety. And when anxiety becomes a part of your daily life, it could mean that your job doesn't support a healthy work-life balance; rather, it encourages office gossip or has unrealistic expectations for its employees. Monster states that one of the best ways to break this cycle is by scheduling relaxation time throughout the day and saying no to multitasking. However, if your boss is micromanaging you to stay at your desk, you may need to clock out of this toxic job for good.

High Blood Pressure

Managers might be tough every now and then, but a toxic manager, WoW! Now that can be detrimental to your health. For example, in a study published in the Journal of Occupational Health Psychology, researchers found that employees who had negative reactions to their bosses also experienced elevated blood pressure that lingered well into the night. Why might this be the case? Well, researchers believe that rumination (aka mentally analyzing a single event over and over again) is at play. But if you're able to separate home and work life, then you may be able to live a healthier life.

Feeling sick

You can become very sick when your immune system shuts down from stress. Because toxic work environments can drive your stress levels high, your job is more inclined to make you very ill. According to The Atlantic, when you experience chronic stress, it can lower the function of your immune system, making you more susceptible to diseases and illnesses. While you might have hand sanitizer at your desk to eliminate germs, there's not enough hand sanitizer in the world to eliminate a toxic work environment.

Paranoia

Toxic work environments breed instability, fear, and uncertainty. But mix that with poor communication, and you'll receive a tall order of paranoia. Poor work cultures will lead employees to assume they'll inevitably lose their jobs because their bosses might make them feel inadequate, or office gossip about the company might plague their thoughts. According to Psychology Today, these tactics can create stress, paranoia, and a feeling of adrenaline, making you feel less confident in yourself.

Negative Outlook

When your office culture goes off the rails, it can be hard not to let it affect your personal life. You're more inclined to engage in negative self-talk and complain about your job when working in a toxic environment. While this can definitely impact your personal relationships, it can also affect your relationship with yourself. When you're not able to pull yourself out of this negative mindset, you have more of a chance to become addicted to drama and behavior, which can be harmful to your health in the long run.

These are but some health-related issues that may affect someone working in a toxic work environment. These are some serious issues that should never be taken lightly. If you are presently in a toxic workplace and your health is affected, it's time to make your exit because it makes no sense to allow yourself to suffer for a job that does not value you as a professional and as a person. The company will replace you; God forbid, if something happens to you, it's as real as that.

This world is overflowing with opportunities, and you should never feel trapped in a job for the sake of a paycheck. Great leaders understand the power inside of them and their infinite abilities, and as such you should never be a slave for a salary because of your greatness. Never let any job affect your health; Your health is your wealth, and the people who truly value you, your husband, wife, children, family and friends, need you to be around for a long time, save your time and energy for them; to help make a difference in this world but never for an employer who cares nothing about you.

4

PLAYING THE GAME: THE DELUSIONAL NATURE OF OFFICE POLITICS

"When there is no consequence for poor work ethic, and no reward for good work ethic, there is no motivation."

I still remember the day someone said to me, "Gifford, you have to learn to play the game." So I am left wondering, what game are you referring to? As a service provider, we have a significant responsibility, and many people rely on us. Therefore, we should prioritize fulfilling our duties rather than engaging in games.

Throughout my career, I am always amazed by the "games" individuals play to advance their interests. Some would call me naïve, but after 15 years of working in various capacities in the public and private sectors, I am still amazed by the extent some people go to promote their agenda. WoW, looking back, I can now understand that if you do not have that shared sense of purpose, people will, unfortunately, have their agenda and will go to lengths to ensure their plan is completed. In a Harvard Business Review article, Tomas Chamorro-Premuzic spoke about the psychological effects of office politics. Sigmund Freud noted that although humans are social animals, living with others does not come easy. He compared people to a group of hedgehogs during the winter: they need to get close to each other to cope with the cold, but if they get too close, they end up stinging each other with their prickly spines.

This very rule governs the dynamic of office politics. You can't go it alone, but working with others does require some discomfort. So, does this mean that office politics are inevitable – that if we can't beat politics, we might as well promote them? Well, that is the delusional nature of office politics; some people believe that you cannot beat them, so join them. I even heard people with good intention state I have bills to pay, so they can do whatever they want once my salary is in the bank at the end of the month.

According to Dana Rousmaniere, nobody likes office politics. In fact, most of us try to avoid it all costs. But the reality is that companies are, by nature, political organizations, which means that if you want to survive and thrive at work, you can't just sit out on the sidelines. If you want to impact your organization, like it or not, you need to learn how to play the game. That doesn't mean you have to play dirty, but you have to figure out how to influence those around you.

But do you really have to play this game? Take this real-life example from Michael Chang Wenderoth, who wrote about this young lady trying to make her mark in her company. A rising young executive found herself strategically ousted in an internal power play. Jill had all the chops to rise to the corner office: consistent top 10% performer, hardworking, intelligent, personable, driven, multilingual, and a postgraduate from a top-tier school. Handwritten thank-you notes from the CEO proudly adorned her wall.

What happened?

When I met Jill (not her real name), she struggled to understand her career setback. "I was universally liked across the company, a team player who put in more hours than anyone else," she said. "I was heads down on delivering results, shared my inner self and built trust...everything I was trained and even coached to do."

According to Michael Chang Wenderoth, with those words, I recognized what had happened immediately. Jill was one more victim of what I call the "Kumbaya" school of leadership, which says that being open, trusting, authentic, and confident — and working really hard — is the key to getting ahead. The Kumbaya school is doing the Jills of the world a great disservice, leading them to often act in ways that are detrimental to their careers.

What should Jill have done differently? Well, according to Michael, Jill should have spent much more time managing up. She should have better-managed decision-makers, her boss, her image, and her own career. Rather than being chained to her desk delivering great work, Jill should have been networking with the most influential executives, ensuring those above her noticed her contributions and confirming that she was being perceived as executive-suite material.

Oh really! So let me get this straight, instead of producing work that helped the organization meet its objectives, being authentic and trustworthy, and being a team player; Jill should have virtually sucked up to the executives to advance her career. That's utterly ridiculous, and if you find yourself in an environment where your work means nothing to the leaders of the organization, you need to find another place to work. No one, not the leadership or junior staff, should accept that type of behavior at their job, but before we get into the approaches and strategies one can use to mitigate these practices at their company, let's look at the negative aspects of office politics and how it can lead to a demotivated workforce.

The Adverse Effects Of Politics

1. Employees who do not believe in working hard depend on nasty politics to secure their workplace position.

2. Employees play politics simply to come into the limelight and gain undue attention and appreciation from the seniors.

3. Politics refers to the irrational behavior of individuals in the workplace to obtain advantages beyond their control.

4. Nobody has ever gained anything out of politics; instead, it leads to a negative ambiance at the workplace.

Source: Management Study Guide

According to Tomas Chamorro-Premuzic, it's important to recognize that untrammeled politics have a corrosive impact on the organization. This can be hard for leaders to realize: because most organizations promote individuals who are politically savvy, managers and senior executives tend to perpetuate rather than inhibit office politics.

If you are rewarded for "playing the game," you surely have no incentive to stop playing. But to most employees, politics signal a discrepancy between what should be done and what is really done, defeating their own sacrifices and efforts. This leaves most employees demoralized and united only against their bosses or senior leadership, which is not a good position for a company to be in.

What Can A Leader Do?

Well, according to Tomas Chamorro-Premuzic, conversely, in less toxic companies, leaders manage the tensions within groups to enhance team performance and, in turn, organizational effectiveness. To do this, the best managers recognize the psychological underpinnings of office politics and do two things in response:

1. They manage the way they themselves behave, and

2. They are careful about how they motivate others.

As such, great leaders focus on the bright-side personality characteristics associated with their ability to navigate office politics: social skills, emotional intelligence, and intuition. They recognize that the more secretive, selfish, hypocritical, hierarchical, and incompetent they appear in the eyes of employees, the more political the organization will become. So, they are driven to genuinely be competent, transparent, approachable and altruistic.

People must understand the influential nature of leadership. As mentioned above, if a leader has questionable tendencies, that organization will be very political. If you have a leader who promotes that type of practice within their company, what do you think will happen? It will become commonplace, and the people who care about their work and believe in putting in the hours and working really hard will eventually become delusional and believe they are doing something wrong. Real leaders motivate and inspire their employees to try harder; they avoid pitting employees against one another and instead focus on outperforming common adversaries: the company's competitors. They do this through articulating a meaningful mission — a vision that resonates and motivates people to achieve a collective goal. This keeps the team focused on achieving their purpose rather than internally fighting with each other. Additionally, Management Study Guide also suggests that the best way to win office politics is to:

- Stay out of it. Don't get involved in any of the controversies at the workplace. Avoid unnecessary disputes and conflicts.

- Focusing on your own tasks is important instead of getting involved in others' affairs. Keep in mind that you're compensated for your diligent efforts, not for engaging in unethical office politics.

- Don't always find faults in others. Try your level best to help your fellow workers whenever needed. Never give them the wrong suggestions.

- Be honest. Never break anyone's trust. If any of your colleagues have confided in you, don't ever walk up to the superiors and disclose the secrets.

For all the people reading this article and for the people who are in that type of environment and believe that's how the world of work is especially the young people, I have news for you; it's not. People who strive in that type of environment are the ones who are:

- Trying to advance their personal agenda.

- They were influenced by that type of behavior during their career and believed that's the norm and

- They are very insecure about their ability to lead.

I have seen these types of behaviors from leaders and their junior staff with my own eyes. This is not normal, and it should be eradicated immediately. Now, before I hyperventilate while writing this chapter, I want to stop at this point. I am strongly against any office politics, and as leaders, we have a responsibility to ensure our employees love their work. Creating a positive and productive workplace should be our priority, instead of one filled with negative behaviors such as gossip, backstabbing, backbiting, and personal attacks on individuals' character.

For those who continue to tell me, "Gifford, office politics is a way of life, accept it." I will continue to respond by stating that no one, especially any leader, should encourage and participate in that behavior; no one should accept that delusional thinking. Maybe in their own little world, that's a norm, but not me; I will continue to advocate against this type of practice and always strive to influence and inspire other leaders to create an excellent organization, one their employees will love and enjoy.

Let's change the leadership status quo.

5

GREAT LEADERS ARE GREAT LISTENERS

"As a leader you should never be too busy to listen because it's the ultimate form of respect anyone can give to another human being."

When you speak in such a way others love listening to you and listen in such a way that others love talking to you. It shows you value your team by actively listening to their concerns, feedback or suggestions. I often wonder why companies ask their employees for their feedback when time and time again, they never listen to what their employees are saying.

Effective leadership is built on a foundation of communication and collaboration; as a result, one crucial aspect of this is listening to your team. Unfortunately, some leaders disregard many of their team's feedback and suggestion, creating an environment of diminished trust, stifled creativity, and decreased productivity.

I can remember during many meetings I attended, the routine was always the same: "Does anyone have any suggestions, feedback or questions for the management team" The CEO always asked when the meeting was coming to a close. Many people always voice their concerns or offer some form of suggestion. Still, nothing came from any of it. I can distinctly remember watching the managers at the front table when people were talking, and no one seemed remotely interested in anything anyone was saying. It was so glaring and so disrespectful. But you know what was ironic? I've heard some of these same managers complain that "my employees won't speak up" and label them as bad or uncaring employees, but these same "leaders" should look in the mirror and ask themselves how their people ended up that way. When someone is sharing their ideas and feedback, and they are not taken seriously, at some point, that person will become very quiet, and the worst thing for any organization is when their most passionate employees become quiet. We will address this further in Chapter 7.

When leaders consistently fail to listen to their teams, trust begins to erode. Team members may feel undervalued, marginalized, and disrespected. This breakdown in trust inhibits open communication and collaboration, as individuals become hesitant to voice their concerns or share their ideas. The resulting lack of transparency and teamwork hinders overall organizational effectiveness. Why would anyone waste their energy to voice anything when no one is listening? They may be hearing, but they don't listen. In Mike Myatt's article Why Most Leaders Need to Shut Up and Listen, Mike indicated that while some people may be impressed with how well you speak, the right people will be impressed with how well you LISTEN.

Great leaders are great listeners, they talk less and listen more, and as a result, they are very proactive, strategic, and intuitive listeners. They recognize knowledge and wisdom are not gained by talking but by listening. According to David Grossman, the most exceptional skill that any leader can master is becoming comfortable with silence. Don't view silence as this empty space that needs to be filled but learn to accept it and work with it; you will be amazed at how your silence opens up doors for others to speak and be heard. The result is often an unexpected and enlightening connection and a wealth of information. When you take the time to listen to someone, really take the time to listen actively; it shows you value the person, which is the ultimate form of respect. If you look bored or interrupt the person, you're showing that you don't really care what they have to say. There is a fundamental difference between passage listening and active listening. According to Key Difference, active listening, as the name suggests, is the process wherein the listener carefully hears what the speaker says, processes the message and then responds to the message to lead the conversation further.

When someone is actively listening, it shows that the person is paying full attention to the speaker, showing interest in what they are saying through expressions, body language and asking questions at timely intervals to make a good conversation. On the other hand, passive listening means listening to the speaker but not paying attention to what the speaker is actually saying. Now let's take a look at how active listening can make you a more effective leader. Active listening involves:

- Giving full attention to the speaker.
- Seeking to understand their perspective.
- Providing feedback that demonstrates understanding.

Leaders can foster active listening by creating an environment where everyone's voice is heard and differing viewpoints are respected. They can also use techniques like paraphrasing, summarizing, and asking clarifying questions to ensure effective comprehension. According to Maggie Wooll, we can always learn from those around us, including our direct reports. Effective listening gives you knowledge and perspectives that increase your leadership capacity. Being open to feedback and new ideas from your team helps you learn and grow as a leader. Genuinely listening to someone as a leader shows you care what they're saying and empathize with their feelings. This creates a work environment of trust, and having your employees' confidence gives you the ability to help everyone on your team become the very best version of themselves. At the same time, it inspires and motivates everyone to be more committed to their work.

You can only become a great leader by being a great communicator. But many leaders believe communication is only about talking. So they talk and talk and talk. They tell people what to think, how to think and when to think. Communication is also about listening. In fact, communication is mostly about listening. Leaders who do listen give themselves a chance to learn. They allow themselves to receive information from multiple sources and break it down into actionable tasks.

Leadership is not only about directing and delegating; it is about building relationships, fostering collaboration, and listening to the voices of those around you. Leaders who fail to listen to their team risk alienating their employees, stifling creativity, and inhibiting growth. On the other hand, leaders who embrace the power of listening can create an environment where everyone feels valued, empowered, and motivated to contribute their best. By prioritizing active listening, fostering trust, and empowering their teams, leaders can cultivate a culture of collaboration, innovation, and success.

Ultimately, the true measure of leadership lies in the ability to listen, understand, and respond to the needs of those being led. Remember, you are the leader; you must set the example because you set the tone for everyone to follow. So, when you are talking with someone, for example, make that person the most important person in the world because it shows a level of respect and appreciation for what the person is actually saying and, in the process, permits others to do the same.

6
GREAT LEADERS ALLOW THEIR TEAM TO DISAGREE WITH THEM, HERE'S WHY

"Good leadership requires you to surround yourself with people of diverse perspectives who can disagree with you without fear of retaliation." - Doris Kearns Goodwin

Leadership is often associated with making decisions, giving directions, and providing guidance. However, truly effective leaders understand the value of fostering an environment where their team members feel comfortable disagreeing with their leader. By encouraging and embracing disagreement, leaders can unlock the potential for growth, innovation, and better decision-making in their team, which ultimately adds value to the company and, by extension, to the people they are entrusted to serve.

Collaboration doesn't always mean everyone agrees with everything, according to Allaya Cooks-Campbell, who wrote a great article on How To Disagree At Work Without Being Obnoxious. There will be times when you will have a difference of opinion, which is perfectly normal; as a matter of fact, it's a great thing. Teams that work together benefit from productive conflict. According to Adam Grant, "If two people always agree, it's a sign that at least one of them isn't thinking critically or speaking candidly. Differences of opinion don't have to be threats. They can be opportunities to learn." Being able to disagree with your colleagues and even your leader is a sign of a psychologically safe workplace. Disagreement is a normal part of any healthy relationship, and that's not the same as conflict. Learning how to disagree respectfully allows you to grow continually as a communicator while, in the process, creating a culture allowing others to do the same.

Great leaders embrace diversity of thought because having diverse people and views on your team helps leaders make better decisions. The most effective teams and organizations regularly disagree. Still, traditional work cultures have conditioned us to think that everyone should agree with everything, and those with any opposing viewpoint are labeled as troublemakers or disruptors. But if everyone's always agreeing, how do you know what people are actually thinking?

No leader should surround themselves with a sea of yes men or women who agree with everything they say and do. To build a great company, you must have some sense of respectful disagreements among your team. We need to create safe work cultures that honor differences of opinion. No one will ever have all of the correct answers, and it's only through conversation, debate, and, yes, even argument those real ideas come out and better decisions are made. I know it can be very disheartening to hear a board member, team member, or employee disagree with your idea or strategy.

However, your job as a leader is to listen to what they have to say, according to Tori Utley. This is very important because no one will ever have all the correct answers, and ultimately, you will make better decisions as a leader by having diverse people and views on your team. But it all starts with the leader and their ability to listen to their team when someone disagrees or offers a different opinion. When someone can raise their hand and say 'I disagree," without any fear of victimization or termination, that indicates that the leader has created a safe environment that allows their team to be themselves. The problem with many organizations is that there are people who sit in leadership positions and expect their team to agree with everything.

These weak leaders take disagreement personally and feel threatened, offended, and attacked when their team challenges their ideas and opinions. They react by waving off disagreement as unimportant, and at worse, they remove those who disagree with them. This ultimately leads to a team of individuals who feel undervalued and uninspired. Leaders should celebrate disagreements and view them as opportunities for growth and learning. When team members engage in respectful debate and present alternative ideas, leaders should acknowledge their contributions and emphasize the importance of divergent thinking. This helps establish a culture where dissent is valued and seen as a catalyst for improvement.

When disagreements arise, they can turn into conflicts that negatively impact productivity and teamwork. Leaders should be equipped to handle emotions and encourage constructive discussions to prevent this. This can be achieved by setting ground rules for respectful communication, encouraging active listening, and mediating conflicts. Implementing these strategies can help leaders maintain a positive and productive environment even when there are differing opinions. While disagreement is essential, leaders must also focus on building consensus and alignment once discussions have taken place. It's very important that leaders facilitate a process that allows for collective decision-making, where differing viewpoints are considered, compromises are explored, and a shared understanding is reached. This ensures that after disagreements, the team can move forward united and committed to the agreed-upon course of action. Leaders who recognize the value of team disagreement create a culture that thrives on diversity of thought, innovation, and effective decision-making. By encouraging people to offer a different point of view leaders can foster an environment where individuals feel safe to express their opinions, challenge assumptions, and contribute to the growth and success of the organization.

Strategies such as cultivating psychological safety, establishing clear communication channels, and implementing structured debates empower teams to collaborate and leverage their collective intelligence. Overcoming challenges related to emotions, power dynamics, and achieving consensus requires strong leadership and a commitment to open dialogue. Ultimately, leaders who embrace team disagreement pave the way for enhanced creativity, stronger relationships, and a more resilient and adaptable organization.

7

WHEN YOUR MOST PASSIONATE EMPLOYEES BECOME QUIET

"The Biggest Concern of any organization should be when their most passionate people become quiet." - Tim McClure

After eight months of working in her new role as a senior associate, Sarah noticed changes within her organization, and it's making her very uncomfortable. Now, if you know Sarah, she loves her job; she is the spark and energy of the room, going the extra mile and dedicated to the company's purpose and vision. But something was changing; the leadership made significant changes within the organization without any input from staff, which affected Sarah immensely.

She tried to offer her feedback, but no one took her seriously. As a result, the organizational culture was slowly shifting from one that was very inspirational and motivational to one that breeds toxicity. Sensing that the organization did not value her work again, Sarah became very disengaged; she kept her head under the radar while looking for a new job, losing all enthusiasm for her job. When passionate employees become quiet, according to Tim McClure, it usually signals that the work environment has become very dysfunctional. Suspicion and insecurity cloud the culture, and employees retreat into self-protection behavior patterns to protect themselves from the forces within the company. Many of the problems existing in varying organizations today come from piss poor leadership and management. While great leaders encourage their employees to reach their full potential and help their organizations surpass their goals, weak managers push their employees away to the point where many jump ship.

According to Greg Savage, most people don't change jobs solely for money. They rarely resign on a whim or in a fit of anger. They joined the company because they believed it was right for them and wanted it to be right. Something, at some point, made it wrong. And if you really take the time to dig into their real reasons for leaving and you should; you will find that it's not "the company" they blame. It's not the location, or the team, or the database or the air-conditioning. It's the leadership! So, next time you get a resignation, resist the temptation to laugh it off as "another dumbo who doesn't get us." It's not the departing employee who doesn't "get it." It's not the company they are leaving; it's the leadership.

As a leader, how do you prevent your most passionate employee from becoming quiet?

You need to look at the organization's leadership as the first order of business because the problems usually start there. People don't lose their motivation and inspiration overnight; it's always a combination of small and big things that creeps into the organization slowly and consistently over time. When leadership operates out of a vague sense of direction with little or no communication of an expected future state, people within the organization will eventually become very disengaged. Significant organizational changes can have a major impact on passionate employees as well. Just like Sarah, they may feel uncertain about the future or disillusioned with the new direction. Again, communication is very important, and as a result, you must be transparent about changes, provide reassurance, and involve employees in the decision-making process whenever possible. Help them see how their passion can contribute to the organization's success in the new landscape.

Remember, each employee is unique, and their reasons for becoming quiet may vary. When you have a team that is passionate, inspired, and motivated to help the company achieve its vision while fulfilling its purpose, you must do everything in your power to ensure that this team keeps this vibe. It is essential to listen actively, show empathy, and address individual concerns. By creating an environment that nurtures passion, autonomy, growth, and open communication, you can help re-ignite their enthusiasm and regain their active participation. Otherwise, you risk pushing away great talent while settling for mediocrity.

8

SIGNS OF A TOXIC WORK CULTURE BOTH LEADERS AND EMPLOYEES CAN LOOK OUT FOR

"The culture of any organization is shaped by the worst behavior the leader is willing to tolerate."

Toxic people are a poison that threatens to contaminate their workplace environment. They spread dissent and discontent among co-workers, lowering employee morale and productivity. These individuals can wreak havoc on any organization, whether manipulators, gossipers, whiners, or backstabbers. Unfortunately, many companies have toxic employees but fail to deal with them.

Sometimes, the elements of a toxic work culture will be right out in the open and so easy to fix; other times, they are hidden, and leaders should make consistent efforts to unearth them. So, if you are a newly minted graduate looking to make your mark in the world or a seasoned professional suspicious of your workplace culture, recognizing the signs of a toxic work culture is crucial for identifying and addressing these issues. Here are some signs that both leaders and employees can look out for:

Low Morale At Work

If you find yourself in a work environment where negativity, rumors, gossip, and backstabbing are prevalent, it's likely that you're dealing with a toxic workplace. This type of environment can lead to ongoing dissatisfaction and exhaustion, and it can also hinder teamwork and trust. As a leader, it's essential to maintain a positive attitude and boost morale. Your positive energy can be highly contagious, spreading throughout your work culture. When your colleagues use respectful language, show warmth, and engage in good-natured humor, it can quickly transform your workplace into a great place to work.

There Is A Lack Of Communication

An unmistakable sign of a toxic work culture is when communication is predominantly top-down, where directives flow only from higher-ups to the employees. This type of work environment often lacks open and honest communication, resulting in critical information being withheld and a lack of transparency between management and employees. For a work culture to thrive, communication must flow in both directions. When employees feel heard and valued, they are more likely to contribute to the success of the company. As leaders let's strive to build open and honest communication channels in our workplaces, where all voices are heard and respected.

Employees Are Afraid Of Their Manager

A toxic work culture is often characterized by employees feeling fearful or threatened by their superiors or colleagues. This can result from behaviors such as intimidation, bullying, or a hostile atmosphere, which can damage trust and create a harmful work environment. A healthy respect for your manager is essential, but being afraid of them is unacceptable. If employees feel too intimidated to express their thoughts during meetings or even avoid interacting with their manager, it indicates a toxic workplace culture. Remember, a leader significantly impacts the overall culture of an organization, and it can either foster a toxic environment or a happy one for their employees.

Insistence On Policies Over People

When there is a lack of consistency in enforcing policies and procedures or when there is a perception of favoritism, it can foster a toxic work culture. This erodes trust and can create a sense of injustice among employees. It is imperative that policies and procedures are enforced with a consistent and fair approach to help create an environment where employees feel secure and respected, but also to ensure that everyone is held to the same standards and expectations. Toxicity occurs when this level of consistency and fairness is eroded, and there is no trust in the organization's leadership. Therefore, it is crucial for leaders to prioritize these aspects of workplace culture and to ensure all employees are treated fairly.

There Is A High Employee Turnover

Frequent employee turnover could be a sign of a toxic work environment especially when employees who feel undervalued, unappreciated, or overwhelmed with stress and pressure. If you find yourself frequently hiring new employees as a result of a high turnover rate, it may be time to examine the culture of your workplace. While it's natural for individuals to seek new opportunities, a consistently high turnover rate can point to underlying issues within the company.

Unhealth Competition

Although competition can be positive in the workplace, it is imperative to recognize when it becomes detrimental to employee wellness. If competition turns into a cutthroat environment where coworkers are consistently competing against one another or are pressured to adopt a win-at-all-costs mentality, it can lead to heightened stress and a hostile atmosphere. These negative effects can significantly impact employee morale and ultimately result in decreased productivity and overall workplace satisfaction. Therefore, it is important to cultivate a healthy competitive culture that encourages teamwork and growth rather than a toxic environment that pits employees against each other.

Micromanagement

Great leaders build great teams and give them the freedom to produce great work because it makes no sense to recruit the best and micromanage their work. Micromanaging employees is a leadership style that can negatively affect their work environment. When leaders constantly monitor and control their employees without trusting them to do their jobs effectively, it often leads to feelings of frustration and demotivation. Empowering employees is a leadership approach that can create a positive impact on the workplace. By showing trust in their abilities and providing your team with the necessary resources, they will feel motivated and productive. A good leader knows when to step back and let their team shine.

Successful companies understand that culture is crucial to their success. They recognize that when problems develop, changes are sometimes necessary to eliminate the toxic behaviors dragging down the company. Outstanding leadership is essential to any organizational success. In some cases, leadership itself may need to make changes, especially if much of the problem can be traced to toxic leadership. When toxic behaviors are tolerated, they can significantly affect the company's culture, decrease collaboration between teams, affect how customers are treated, and so much more. People in leadership positions often look for a quick fix, but it's not that simple. It's easy to blame the hiring process or one employee, but unfortunately, the buck stops with you as the person sitting in the leadership position. You need to take full responsibility for the low morale of your department or organization and urgently address the situation before all the good employees leave and the toxic remains.

Ask yourself these questions:

•Has the company moved away from its purpose and vision?

•Is there open and honest communication to reinforce the company's purpose, vision, and values?

•Has the leadership stayed true to the company's values by leading by example?

•What about empathy? Does the leadership value empathy and recognize this as a critical aspect of their leadership?

You cannot stamp out toxicity in your company if the leadership is toxic; as the leader you must inspire change and demonstrate an unwavering commitment and willingness to eliminate all traces of toxic behavior in their leadership first because this will set an example for everyone to follow. In the follow chapters we will look at how you can use communication to inspire change in your organization because communication is one of the potent antidote any leader can use to mitigate toxicity and bring about inspirational, genuine, motivational, and positive change in their organization successfully.

PART TWO

USING COMMUNICATION TO INSPRIE CHANGE

9

THE INTRO

"The art of communication is the language of leadership." - James Humes

Inspiration comes in many forms; song, poetry, movies, experiences, and many more. However, the underlying conduit for all inspiration is communication. Some leaders, for example, have a gift of motivating and inspiring people to believe in the impossible. When someone feels inspired, they become confident, feel important, and they automatically see solutions instead of problems, and that feeling somehow spreads to others.

For some, it comes naturally, but others must work consistently to improve their communication skills because a skilled communicator can influence many people positively or negatively. For example, many leaders have taken companies close to bankruptcy and turned things around to the astonishment of many people, especially the naysayers who predicted the company's end.

Four leaders immediately come to mind Steve Jobs, Howard Schultz, Anne Mulcahy and Alan Mulally. They achieved the impossible by inspiring their team to believe in their vision for the company. Let's look at these four companies a bit more in detail, and you will understand the magnitude of their problems before the transformation.

Ford

In 2007, Ford was in severe trouble and closed to bankruptcy when Alan Mulally became the company's CEO. To put Ford's position in context, listed below were some of the problems the company was facing:

- The company lost 12 billion dollars in 2006.
- The demand for their vehicles declined rapidly.
- Their share price was at the lowest rate ever.
- The culture of the company was nauseatingly toxic.
- Staff morale was the lowest it had ever been.
- There was no synergy among the various business units in the world, and the company ultimately lost its focus.

The above description looks daunting, and you may be wondering who, within their right mind, would take on such a responsibility to turn around a company that lost 12 billion dollars in one-year, hemorrhaging cash at an alarming rate. This was the situation at Ford in 2006, on the brink of bankruptcy and feverishly looking for someone to help turn things around.

Starbucks

In 2008, Starbucks was forced to close 600 stores in the US, their profit fell by 28 percent, and in 2009, it closed another 300 stores and laid off 6,700 employees. The situation looked hopeless, with many people predicting that Starbucks would soon close its doors permanently in the near future. However, things turned out completely different.

Apple

In 1986, this once iconic company became the laughing stock of the world. The once-mighty Apple was dead in the water, with Wall Street analysts even predicting the end of Apple to the point where Apple was practically giving away its shares.

Xerox

In 2001, Xerox had over $17 billion in debt and recorded losses in each of the preceding six years. Anne Mulcahy was named CEO of Xerox Corp to lead the turnaround; However, Mulcahy was not ready for such a responsibility, but she was expected to reverse the company's fortunes after a sustained period of underperformance.

Four companies, four completely different industries, four different leaders, and four different leadership styles, but with one commonality; All these leaders who led these incredible comebacks used communication to lead the transformation of their companies. Communication was that vital link that allowed the transformation to become successful. These companies got a new awakening, and these four cases immediately come to mind.

Interestingly, I spent close to a year conducting research and investigating the communication strategies of a company involved in a transformational change. Now, one would think that this relatively small company will not have the same problems as a large company like Ford or Apple, but the similarities were quite glaring. The company had about 200 employees. The investigation unearthed a series of problems because management traditionally overlooked communication as an essential vehicle to augment change and, more importantly, a strategy to inspire and motivate their employees about the change. I felt the emotion when I spoke to the employees because the word change alone invokes a sense of fear in the hearts of many people. As a result, the lack of a coherent communication strategy made the process very confusing for many people at that company. The change was derailed because communication was not a prominent feature. According to John P. Kotter, a common theme across the literature indicates that this type of change is hard to achieve, with more than 70% of transformational change programs failing. John P. Kotter made this assertion years ago, and believe it or not, these issues are still relevant today.

I am always left dumbfounded when people who sit in leadership positions are pretty happy to follow the status quo and allow their organization to fall into an abyss during any change, given the expanse of literature available. Kotter further argued that over 100 companies try to remake themselves into significantly better companies; however, a few of these corporate change efforts have been very successful; but some have been utter failures in most instances.

Some companies have successfully implemented change throughout the length and breadth of their organization, so this begs the question, what is the secret behind a successful transformational change, and why do leaders identify communication as an integral component of the change process? Any company, regardless of its size, location, industry or sector, will be involved in some form of change. It is inevitable. The world is extremely dynamic, and as the leader, you will have the responsibility to lead the change by example. As the leader, you must understand the crucial role communication plays during the change process because, ultimately, it will determine if your change efforts are successful. It's not rocket science; it has been done before. When you are armed with the knowledge, understanding, and application of communication in a changing environment, you will become a dynamic, motivating and inspirational leader who can lead any change successfully.

10

WHY COMMUNICATION IS SO VITAL DURING A CHANGE

"The single biggest problem in communication is the illusion that it has taken place." – George Bernard Shaw.

From 1992 to 2007, Starbucks was the darling of Wall Street. The company experienced unprecedented growth and won numerous awards such as "Best Business," "Most Admired Company," "100 Best Corporate Citizens," and many more. Then, in 2007, a leaked memo from Starbucks chairman Howard Schultz alluded to the fracturing of Starbucks' soul and boom; in the middle of the worse financial meltdown since the great depression, the company's profit plummeted.

The following year, 2008, Starbucks was forced to close 600 stores in the U.S., its profit fell 28 percent, and in 2009, it closed another 300 stores and laid off 6,700 employees. During that time, the company's Chairman, Howard Schultz, returned as CEO to lead the transformation and return the company to its glory days. One of Schulz's primary weapons used in the turnaround of Starbucks was communication and it came as a surprise to many people in and out of the company when Schulz took 10,000 store managers to New Orleans for a conference; yes, 10,000 managers in the midst of the worst time in the company's history. Many people did not understand his decision, but Schultz knew that if people were reminded of the company's character and values, everyone could make a difference.

The conference was about galvanizing the company's entire leadership, being vulnerable and transparent with their employees about how desperate the situation was and making them understand that everyone must be personally accountable and responsible for every customer interaction. Schulz used his strength as an excellent communicator to galvanize support for the turnaround of Starbucks and it started with that emotional reconnection with the values of the company by the leadership. Howard Schultz inspired everyone at Starbucks to believe in the company's core purpose again.

As a result, the company experienced a resurgence, surpassing all its company projections, cementing its status as the leader in their industry and one of the most recognizable brands in the world. The lesson to be learned from the Starbucks experience is this; when you are leading a change, you must have an appreciation for communication; as a matter of fact, your plan will undoubtedly fail if communication is not an integral aspect of your change. According to Johnson, Scholes, and Whittington (2008), managers faced with effecting change typically underestimate substantially the extent to which members of the organization understand the need for change, what is intended to achieve or what is involved in the change.

Leading change requires using diverse communication techniques to deliver appropriate messages, assure understanding, solicit feedback, create readiness, provide a sense of urgency, and motivate recipients to act. Leaders are responsible for communicating to the organization the risks of clinging to the status quo and the potential rewards of embracing a radically different future. In addition, communication can be an effective tool for motivating employees involved in the change. Appropriate communications provide employees with feedback and reinforcement during the change, enabling management to make better decisions while helping prepare the organization for the advantages and disadvantages to follow.

Research has proven that the entire change process may turn into a fiasco without a proper communication plan. Emerald Research indicated that poorly managed change communication results in rumors and resistance to change which can exaggerate the negative aspects of the change. The empirical picture that is slowly emerging indicates that your communication plan and organizational change implementation are inextricably linked processes.

Any company's change effort depends on the organization's ability to change the individual behaviour of an employee. Therefore, communication with these employees should be an important and integrative part of the change efforts and strategies. One of the primary purposes of change communication should be to inform your team about the change and how their work is altered due to the change.

This informative function of communication will affect your readiness for change. In Jon Wolper's article, Making Change Successful, Robert Half Management Resources survey indicated that 46 percent of change management efforts fail during execution. The reason, very often, is a lack of clear communication. "Communication is always the thing, for one reason or another, that seems to struggle through the execution stage," says Tim Hird, executive director of Robert Half Management Resources. In the survey, 65 percent of respondents said that communicating clearly, openly and frequently is the most critical action to take when going through organizational change. However, the survey also found that small companies were more susceptible to failure during the execution stage of their change. More than 48 percent of companies with 20-99 employees indicated that communication is the primary issue compared with just 29 percent of companies with more than 1,000 employees.

Good organizational communication is a crucial factor in effectively managing people. However, communication takes on a more significant role during any change process simply because communication reduces uncertainty and also increases a sense of control over personal circumstances related to change and job satisfaction, according to Bordia et al. (2004). In 2001, Anne Mulcahy was named CEO of Xerox Corp, responsible for leading a company on the edge of bankruptcy. Xerox had over **$17 billion** in debt and recorded losses in each of the preceding six years. Mulcahy said: "I was not ready to lead, let alone the one who was expected to reverse the company's fortunes after a sustained period of underperformance."

Wall Street also agreed; on the day Mulcahy was announced as the CEO, Xerox stock dropped 15 percent, "a real confidence builder," she joked. But Mulcahy soon silenced her critics and led one of the most remarkable turnarounds in corporate history. According to Knowledge @ Wharton, under her leadership, Xerox moved from losing $273 million in 2000 to earning $91 million in 2003. In 2004, the company's profits had reached $859 million on sales of $15.7 billion. At the same time, its stock had risen, returning 75% over the last five years, compared with a loss of 6% for the Dow Jones Total Stock Market Index. Xerox's fortunes changed significantly, and Mulcahy credited communication for the turnaround. According to Insights by Stanford Business, Mulcahy indicated that effective communication was perhaps the single most crucial component of the company's successful turnaround strategy.

"I feel like my title should be Chief Communication Officer because that's really what I do," she said, emphasizing the importance of listening to customers and employees."

Open and honest communication with employees and customers helped Mulcahy identify the problems at Xerox, which was a critical component of their transformational strategies.

Communicating the Why!

In Simon Sinek's now famous Ted Talk, How Great Leaders Inspire Action, Sinek provided a simple but powerful model for inspirational leadership: the golden circle and the question "Why?"

According to Sinek, the fundamental difference between the "Apples" of the world and everyone else is that they start with "why." Because Apple starts with "why" when defining their company, they can attract customers who share their fundamental beliefs. As Sinek puts it, "People don't buy what you do. They buy why you do it." Any successful change begins with answering one of the most fundamental questions about change: Why? It is human nature to understand the reasoning behind an action or a necessary change. Therefore, management should clearly explain the business drivers or opportunities that have resulted in the need for change. It also means addressing why a change is needed now and explaining the risk of not changing. Schultz achieved this in New Orleans when he clearly communicated to all the 10,000 managers the risk of clinging to the status quo; even though the conference cost the company about 30 million dollars, this solidified how important the conference was to Howard Schultz. Communication in a changing environment is one of the most critical variables one must consider when initiating a change. According to Hiatt (2006), employees want to hear why the change is occurring and how the change aligns with the organization's vision from the business leaders.

Therefore, explaining the why is absolutely important even if it costs 30 million dollars. Appropriate communication will significantly help employees understand the reasons for the change and the impact the change will have on them. This is the first requirement if the transformation has any chance of success. Many experts indicated that communication is indispensable when persuading people to support change. Some researchers have even claimed that the essence of change is communication. The first questions people want answered are:

- Why are we making this change?
- Why now?
- How will this change improve things?
- What's wrong with the status quo?
- How will this change affect me?

One of the main components of a successful communication strategy is the selection of appropriate communication channels. In the next chapter, we will explore the various communication channels and how the change complexity or the lack thereof, will determine what channels are best suited for the success of the change.

11
COMMUNICATION CHANNELS

"When trying to achieve any change, your communication channels are critical."

All employees must see the overall picture of what the organization is trying to achieve. So, the question we will be answering now is this, what communication channel is best suited to explain the why and how to keep staff informed about the change to allay their fears and concerns to keep your team inspired and motivated throughout the process. When Steve Jobs returned as the CEO of Apple in 1987, Jobs presented the 'Think Different' campaign for the first time to Apple staff. Do you remember the Think Different ad,

"This is for the crazy ones, the misfits, the square pegs in a round hole,"

You can check it out on YouTube, Think Different was a brilliant mantra used by Jobs and his team to turn around Apple. Jobs spoke with so much emotion and sincerity; explaining at length why Apple became one of the most valuable brands in the world and also explained the benefits and consequences if the company did not change. Harvard University Professor John P. Kotter indicated that poor communication is the root cause of many failed change efforts in many organizations, and without a lot of credible communication, employees' hearts and minds are never captured. As a result, organizations who continually adopt this practice will continue to experience problems during any change process. When trying to achieve any change, your communication channels are critical. It can literally make or break your process; as a result, significant thought should go into its execution, especially during your planning and streamlining of the change. Therefore, let's explore the various communication channels and how the nature of the change will determine what communication channel is most appropriate.

Types of Communication Channels

Face To Face Communication

- Team Briefing
- Conferences
- Presentations and Speeches
- One to One Meeting

Audio Conferencing

- Video Conferencing
- Video/DVD
- Business TV

Print-Based

- Circulars and Memos
- Magazines and Newsletter
- Manuals and Handbook
- Brochures and Report

Computer Based Communication

- Emails
- Intranet
- Corporate Portals

Social Media

- Enterprise Social Networks
- Blogs
- Wikis
- Slack
- Spark
- Flipgrid
- Slack
- WhatApp
- Instagram
- YouTube
- Linkedin

In my investigation I found some very startling management practices during the change. One of the more glaring occurrences was the passiveness in which management communicated with their staff. But what was even more astounding is the fact that management did not employ multiple channels of communication to disseminate information to staff about the change but continued to use a general staff meeting as the main channel of communication to outline the change process. From the interviews conducted all the interviewees agreed that the use of this general staff meeting to outline the upcoming changes was not ideal since the forum was quite inadequate for disseminating any real information about the change. Incorporating a variety of communication channels during the change will ensure that every employee receives the message from management. Individuals will react to change differently and, in the process, contribute to the change based on their degree of information received.

Balogun and Hope Hailey (1999) state that many communication strategies employ different communication mediums since participants will never remember everything from one communication channel during a transformational change. Thus, other mediums can provide a useful backup, such as using reference material for a different group of employees to give further understanding to employees who may be confused about the change.

Some staff requires a richer form of communication (we will address this later), and the responsibility lies with the organization's leadership to simplify the message and tailor what is communicated to staff. Nevertheless, effective communication channels are a vital tool one can use to reinforce senior management's commitment to employees during the change process and alleviate any confusion in employees' minds about a pending or ongoing change.

Your change complexity will determine what channels of communication are suitable or required. Additionally, to build that awareness in the company, the right communication channels must be used. One of the early indicators that a problem existed at the company I investigated was the lack of awareness of the change and the lack of excitement among staff. Some staff was not aware of the change. As a result, an effective communication channel is a critical component one must employ to create that awareness among all employees to ensure the change is successful.

Choosing The Right Channels

When planning your change, the key to choosing a communication channel, according to Balogun and Hope Hailey (1999), is to match it to the audience's needs. Non-routine, complex change requires a richer form of message and meaning; for example, face-to-face and interactive channels, as mentioned above, have a more significant impact than any other single medium. These rich channels allow for:

- Rapid feedback.
- A high level of intimacy between employees and management.
- Quick adaptation to employee concerns, in which management can directly respond to signals (mimic and gesture) from employees.

Face-to-face communication allows participants to pick up non-verbal cues as the interaction unfolds, adds richness to the message, and communicates emotional aspects of the communication that otherwise might be hidden. Remember how Steve Jobs communicated with emotion when he spoke to his employees about the "Think Different" campaign. That emotional aspect of the communication is vital because it allowed his team to see and, most importantly, feel his emotion.

That message was so rich and transparent; it was felt by everyone in that room and anyone watching via video. Face-to-face communication also clarifies ambiguities and, according to O'Connor (1990), provides the opportunity for immediate feedback to correct deficiencies that may occur in the communication process. Regardless of your company's path of change during its transformational journey, as mentioned above in fig 2, face-to-face communication should be your primary option, with useful backup from other channels. If you are leading a transformational change or if you are making significant changes in your organisation your communication cannot be routine.

According to Johnson, Scholes, and Whittington (2005), to communicate a highly complex set of changes, it would be inappropriate to use standardized bulletins and circulars. One routine channel of communication to outline a complex change is inadequate; there must be follow-up and avenues for staff to give and solicit feedback about the change from management, particularly if the changes to be introduced are very challenging.

It is essential to decide which channel is best suited to the audience and the message being delivered when leading change. You need to match the communication channel strategy to the context of the design choices. For example, if the changing style is communication and education, then there may be a need to have seminars or training education to make staff aware of the changes. It is important to note that adopting face-to-face as the only mode of communication can be very detrimental to the whole process as well.

Face-to-face communication does not obviate the need for other communication efforts. Although this form of communication channel clearly has its advantages, solely adopting this medium can prove to be very harmful during a complex or transformational change. Moreover, and this is very important, adopting a rich form of communication, like face-to-face meetings for routine change, will confuse the hell out of your employees and waste a lot of time. But, on the flip side, if you adopt a routine form of communication during a complex change, it will lead to mistrust and a lack of awareness about the change. Removing a damaged chair and replacing it with a new one does not require a face-to-face meeting; that's wasting time and energy. Instead, that information can simply be conveyed by email. However, changing the strategic focus, culture, or structure of a company will require a face-to-face meeting and other forms of communication to provide clarity and more details.

Social Media

Social media is a valuable "vehicle" any organization can use to communicate their change effort to their teams because we spend nearly three hours per day on social platforms. In addition, more than half of employers are already using internal social media, and as such, many companies have an opportunity to leverage social media as a significant change management tool. According to a recent study by Weber Shandwick conducted in partnership with KRC Research, 55% of respondents who had gone through a change event at work said they wished their employer offered more digital and social engagement, while 42% said they wanted more face-to-face communication.

Whether companies are using enterprise social networks like blogs, wikis, or platforms like Slack, Spark, and Flipgrid, companies can leverage these social media platforms to help manage the change in their organization. In addition, internal social media can help flatten the organization and drive transparent dialogue across levels, functions, and geographies. When longtime Cisco CEO John Chambers stepped down to serve as chairman in July 2015, the new CEO, Chuck Robbins, along with John Chambers, started two simultaneous Jive threads. One invited employees to thank John, and

another sought feedback from the company employees, "What advice or suggestions do you have for Chuck Robbins as he transitions to CEO?"
The two posts drew over 1,000 comments and over 20,000 views within four days. Similar employee crowdsourcing efforts have been used to redefine company values (at IBM) and generate ideas for cutting operational costs (at BASF). It may no longer be an option for management to ignore social media when managing change; the potential benefits are too substantial to ignore! However, there is also no need to get overly technical. By leveraging your existing platforms and getting creative with platforms like Slack, WhatsApp, Instagram, YouTube, LinkedIn or whatever is appropriate to your organization and the particular change project, you can breathe new life into how you manage change.

It's important to note that social media alone won't increase employee engagement during change. Face-to-face communication, manager's support, and real-time coaching are all critical to preserving trust and boosting morale and performance in times of change. But social media is fast becoming an indispensable supplement. Research has shown that 88% of employees use at least one social media at home and that many want a similar experience at work. It's clear that social is becoming a critical component of any change plan. For example, consider Zappos' former CEO, Tony Hsieh, who announced layoffs for 8% of the company's workforce on Zappos' external blog immediately after sending an internal email.

Employees appreciated the transparency and later engaged with Tony, each other, and Zappos' stakeholders over Twitter. The open conversation provided Zappos with insight into how best to handle sensitive situations, fostered thoughtful, public interaction between management and employees, and even helped some laid-off workers find future employment with other companies. Social media cannot be ignored, but as a leader, you must ensure that you don't let employees post harmful and hurtful messages about others, according to Dr. Carol A. Beatty. Many organizations have found that employee productivity can decrease when they spend too much time on social media. Communication success will occur when rich media is used for non-routine change, and routine communication is used for routine change. One must agree that general communication is critical for a successful change process; the richness of face-to-face communication is undeniable; however, it is absolutely necessary to decide which channel is best suited to the audience and the message being delivered.

12

MAINTAINING CONSISTENCY IN YOUR MESSAGE

"Endlessly repeat the message and have consistency with the message."

As a leader it is vital to endlessly repeat the message of the change and never believe that your staff has heard it too many times, especially during a transformational or complex change. One cannot assume that communicating the change once or twice via many communication channels is sufficient. Even if staff understood the change or have a deep-seated understanding of the change process, continuous repetition is critical to get buy-in from the team while communicating continuously. When Alan Mulally arrived at Ford as the CEO, one of his priorities was identifying Ford's core purpose and charting a vision for Ford's recovery. Mulally found an ad from 1925 in which Henry Ford outlined his purpose for the company:

"Opening the highways for all mankind."

Mulally had that ad blown up and mounted on his wall. Then, he passed out copies to each of Ford's top executives. Mulally made sure that all future product decisions would be weighed against that promise. The core purpose was used as the guiding light for the company and reignited the fire that somehow got extinguished. Ford required a change of focus, vision, strategy, and culture. The glue that held all the components together inside and outside the company was communication. The team developed their One Ford Plan, which became the reference point for the transformation. Mulally had this plan printed on wallet cards and distributed to every Ford employee. He opened every weekly meeting by reviewing them.

He recited them in every speech, town hall meeting, and press conference. One of the most critical variables used to achieve the transformation was a compelling vision, clarity of strategy, open and honest communication, and a change of values. Mulally ensured that his communication was constant and consistent to the point where people got fed up with hearing the four-point plan.

Mulally went to lengths to communicate, make people feel comfortable about the change, and explain their role in the process. One of the most notable illustrations of this point may relate to the fact that Mulally had managed to move his office from the top floor to the fourth floor, where engineers were based, so that he could be available for communication and provide a more 'hands-on' approach. During the change implementation period, there were frequent occasions when Mulally would respond to emails from employees by attending their offices in person or calling them to discuss relevant issues (Hoffman, 2012).

His positive influence over the company eventually caught on; when you have open and honest communication in your business, it will remove any ambiguity and allow your employees to trust the plan, trust the process, and, most importantly, trust the leader. Effective communication means identifying your stakeholders, tailoring your communication, endlessly repeating the message, and having consistency with the message with all stakeholders. It's very important to repeat critical messages several times. The first time you announce a change to employees, they often wonder how it will impact them. You want to ensure your key messages make an imprint in your employee's subconscious minds, but to get this result, you must share the message more often than you think you need to.

For example, have you ever done anything throughout your day on complete auto-pilot? Simple tasks that you get done without thinking about, your subconscious mind is responsible for that automatic behavior like your habits, and it takes over routine tasks and helps you to do them automatically. Picture it like this; your subconscious mind is like a vast memory bank. Its capacity is virtually unlimited, and it permanently stores everything that ever happens to you. By the time you reach the age of 21, you have already permanently stored more than one hundred times the contents of the entire Encyclopedia Britannica.

It has memorized all your comfort zones, and it works to keep you in them. Every time you try to create a new habit, your subconscious pulls you right back to what is familiar. Try this experiment, hold your palm up in front of your face and imagine that you have a lemon on your right palm before your eyes. Do you experience your mouth watering? The conscious mind knows that there is no lemon and it's only your imagination. The subconscious mind is illogical and immediately believes the imaginary data put in your mind, and as a result, your mouth waters.

Put simply, what you focus on, you attract. Any thought that is repeated over and over again will take an imprint on the subconscious mind. It's the same with your communication. Your message will eventually take an imprint on your employee's subconscious mind when it is repeated over and over again. New behaviours will start to manifest to the point where it becomes a habit. Additionally, the consistency of that message is vitally important. In Dr. Lily Cheng's research on the 9 Enablers of Change, the Consistency of Change Message was identified as one of the main enablers to change.

According to the research, maintaining the consistency of the message ensures alignment across the change team, making sure that only "one voice" or "same language" is being spoken. The consistency in the message would also help implement change successfully by reducing ambiguity and confusion. As the leader you should hold regular sessions with your team to allay their fears of the change and continuously explain how the team fits into the overall strategic plan of the organization while maintaining consistency in your message.

13

TOP LEADERSHIP COMMITMENT AND A LINE MANAGER'S ROLE

"If a leader expects their employees to buy into the change, they must be the role models for that change."

Line managers are a crucial bridge between top management and junior members of the organization. Why! Because they are in touch with the day-to-day routines of the organization, which can so quickly become blockages to change. They are in a position to translate change initiatives into a locally relevant form of message, according to Johnson, Scholes, and Whittington (2005).

Line managers' one-to-one communication with staff during a significant change is vitally important. In the absence of this form of communication from their line manager, employees can become extremely confused. One must understand that change engenders fear regardless of the circumstance, and some people are very wary of change. Without that communication from their line manager, an employee's resistance to the change is very high. Managers, therefore, can contribute significantly to galvanizing commitment or add to the resistance and cause a blockage of the change. When a change is ongoing, a manager or supervisor is in the best position to help employees understand the reason for the change. Additionally, managers should discuss the change with their employees through face-to-face communication, employing one-on-one sessions and group meetings. It is worth mentioning again that an employee's manager will help reinforce the change immensely using an active communication channel, especially in the initial stages of a transformational change. One-to-one communication has always proven to be very appropriate since managers can help ease the confusion which may occur but, more importantly, provide that degree of certainty that the change will benefit the organization strategically.

During a change, your line managers must be that principal change agent. So, what is a change agent? A change agent is an individual or group that helps effect change in an organization, and as a result, the change agent is seen as the one or group that motivates, inspires, and leads the change by example, with the intention to influence a positive outlook of the change.
If staff recognizes that their manager or the leadership has no apparent interest in the change, it will automatically filter down to the team that the change is not that important.

This was quite apparent from my investigation. The fact that the general staff meeting was the only communication channel used during the change and managers were unaware of the details of the change indicated to staff that this change was not important. It is worth mentioning that the culture of the organization, but more specifically the leadership culture, facilitated this lack of communication, which contributed significantly towards the communication crisis that occurred at the company.

Leadership Culture

A company's culture is directly influenced by the leader, feeding off the urgency of the leadership team. A culture change should be a priority if management wants to create a new approach to communicating with staff. Well-established routines can be a severe blockage to change. When Mulally arrived at Ford, one of his first acts as CEO was shattering the traditional management culture. Mulally invested significantly in formulating a clear vision for the Ford brand by soliciting the company stakeholders to share the One Ford vision. Mulally's communication with his team and his high level of personal engagement helped make the change at Ford very successful. Mulally was always equipped with optimism and a smile throughout the difficult period at Ford; this proved to be instrumental in improving employee morale and productivity.

Moreover, Mulally has efficiently served as the principal change agent for Ford Motor Company by communicating the reasons and benefits of each change proposal to company stakeholders. For example, selling all company corporate jets but one and minimizing other perks for top executives, including himself, during cost-saving initiatives (Gallo, 2012). This illustrated Mulally's strong commitment to the changes that were being implemented.

Significantly, change proposals drafted and implemented by Mulally met minimum resistance from employees at all levels, even though many workforce members were significantly disadvantaged by the changes. This achievement can be explained through the display of charisma, outstanding leadership skills, and Mulally's practical communication approach. According to Schein (1992), organizational culture is a direct result of a leader's behavior and values, but more importantly, leadership values are crucial to understanding corporate behavior since people tend to emulate the behavior of their leaders with the assumption that their behavior is correct. Role modeling is an effective strategy to facilitate change; however, leaders must be prepared to walk the talk of change to instill any credibility during the change process. In addition, it is important to note that an ill-defined leadership culture can create unclear cues for what is important (purpose and task focus) and how employees should act as it relates to the organization's culture. If the leadership expect employees to buy into the change, they must be the role models for that change. They must lead by example and create a culture that allows employees to accept the changes in the organization.

Managers are a filter of information regarding imminent change, but more importantly, the communication of this information should be relevant and understandable to their employees. One can clearly deduce that a CEO's role, and a line manager's role during the unfreeze, move, and sustain process, is critical to ensure that employees understand their roles since insufficient follow-up and a lack of fine-tuning once implementation begins can lead to resistance from staff.

In many instances there is a direct correlation between the lack of communication and the significantly heightened level of resistance during the any change. Change must be anchored firmly in the organizational culture to last and continuously work on throughout the transformational journey to attain any success. However, to accomplish this, communication must be central to an organization's success.

Line managers, in many instances, are more appropriate to translate change, but top leadership should set the example. Therefore, the line manager's role becomes extremely important where this is concerned. During my investigation, that supervisor-subordinate, two-way communicative process was missing. As a result, some line managers were very skeptical of the changes taking place, and as a result, the management team was not unified in their position about the change, which also created many problems. If the line managers, who are responsible for disseminating information about the change and are considered the principal change agents within their department, do not buy into the change, there will be a communication breakdown in the respective unit and, by extension, the company.

The departmental manager's role in the change solicited some fascinating comments from the interviewees. For example, one interviewee indicated that:

"Managers were not aware of the details of the change."

When asked further about the interviewee's experience in any meeting with their manager, it was pretty surprising to learn that the information was inconsistent with the information coming from the general staff meeting. Again, I need to emphasize this point, the line managers are more appropriate to translate change into language and terminology that is relevant to their staff, but if these managers are limited in their knowledge of the change or don't agree with the change or have concerns about the change, it will create a culture of mistrust and confusion.

In the initial stages of a transformational change, it is essential that managers provide that rich form of communication since this is critical to the whole change process. But for some strange reason, this was never done by the various departmental managers and this created heighten level of resistance throughout the process. As the manager, you have to be on point with your message, especially during a change; any element of inconsistency will spark rumors and confusion in the minds of your employees. From my investigation, management failed to recognize the established norms at the agency and the role culture played during the change process. Management placed more emphasis on changing the structure, systems, and processes at the company, as opposed to the cultural element in the organization. The introduction of structural changes only scratches the surface of any transformation effort, according to Kets de Vries*, Guillén Ramo, and Korotov of INSEAD (2009). Furthermore, because a significant amount of behavior takes place at an unconscious level, mindset changes are not easily accomplished. As a result, the organization's strategic objectives are not achieved.

The CEO should empower their team of line managers and hold them accountable for their actions, especially the communication with staff. A communication audit should be initiated to ensure that the correct information is disseminated to staff. Managers need to be more involved in the change with some degree of accountability; however, this can only happen if there is some form of culture change and cohesion at the leadership level of the organization. A good friend, Mike Manes from Square One Consulting, uses this presentation to show leaders that a cohesive management team is necessary to achieve successful change.

In the presentation, Mike held a dollar bill in one hand and 100 pennies in the other. Mike explained that each hand holds a dollar – they have equal value. They can buy the same things; however, if you toss the dollar bill in the air and let it float to the ground, the dollar is easy to pick up – it is a single unit. If you throw the pennies in the air – you get CHAOS. Leaders too often begin transformational change before they create a cohesive team with a shared PURPOSE, VISION, VALUES, AND MISSION, resulting in a very challenging and, in many instances, failure of any change process.

14

FORMAL OR INFORMAL COMMUNICATION

"When information about a change is inconsistent, people tend to resist it."

Before Howard Schultz announced to the world that he was returning as the CEO of Starbucks, Schultz told one person, his friend Michael Dell. While on a bike ride, Dell indicated to Schultz that he should develop a transformative agenda outlining the change from start to finish and communicating that plan to all the employees at Starbucks. It was a similar situation with Dell a year before when he returned as the CEO of the company he founded. On January 6th, 2008, Howard Schultz wrote a letter to all the partners at Starbucks announcing his return as the CEO of Starbucks. In the letter, Schultz outlined the purpose of the change, the objectives, and the series of activities that led to the fracturing of the Starbucks spirit.

Schultz indicated, and I quote:

"Twenty-five years ago, I walked into Starbucks first store in Seattle's Pike Place Market, and from that day forward we have taken the road less traveled. Working with an exceptional group of people and summoning all the courage we could muster, we created a new kind of place ? one that served the kind of coffee that most people had never tasted, an environment that didn't look like any other store, and hiring people who were fanatically passionate about coffee and celebrated their interaction with customers. To do this, we focused every ounce of our beings on creativity and innovation.

Over the years, together we have built one of the most recognized and respected brands in the world. When we went public in June 1992, we had 119 stores. We now have more than 15,000 stores and a significant and growing presence in 43 countries, serving 50 million customers a week. These customers have placed their trust in us, and for them and for each other we need to ensure that our future is as exciting as our past.

If we take an honest look at Starbucks today, then we know that we are emerging from a period in which we invested in infrastructure ahead of the growth curve. Although necessary, it led to bureaucracy. We will now shift our emphasis back onto customer-facing initiatives, better aligning our back-end costs with our business model. We are fortunate, though, that the challenge we face is one of our own making. Because of this, we know what needs to be done to ensure our long-term future success around the world.

Transforming the *Starbucks Experience*

The Board decided that I should lead this transformation. Given this, effective immediately, in addition to my existing role as chairman, I have returned as chief executive officer for the long-term. Jim Donald is leaving the Company. I want to pay tribute to Jim's leadership. He was a passionate and tireless advocate for Starbucks, and his contribution to our company cannot be overstated. Looking ahead, the reality we face is both challenging and exciting. It's challenging because there are no overnight fixes. Rather, our success will come in the rigorous execution of several new strategic initiatives ? that capitalize on our heritage to drive our successful future. And our reality is exciting because there is so much opportunity ahead for Starbucks."

Source: **Howard Schultz Transformation Agenda Communication #1**

Schultz's letter removed any speculation and rumors about Starbucks' transformation, but more importantly, he ensured that his communication was formal to all employees. When you don't communicate during a change, especially in the early stages, people will start making up their information. They challenge the goals and criticize the change process while imagining the worst that can happen and believing their unrealistic assumptions. As a result, rumors run rampant, and they spread like wildfire.

When leading a change, you must communicate early, often and right through to the end of the change initiative; however, you must limit the informal communication channels, especially grapevine communication, because this can potentially create an environment of miscommunication that can derail the entire process. Grapevine communication cannot be substantiated in any real way. From my investigation, many interviewees kept repeating that the grapevine was their primary source of information during the change. The information from the general staff meetings was extraordinarily inadequate, and without any information from the departmental meetings, the grapevine filled the void.

When information about a change is inconsistent, people tend to resist it. It's important that employees receive information about any new change developments through formal communication channels rather than via the grapevine, which can be unreliable. It is very alarming that any company will value grapevine communication as opposed to formal communication. If you are communicating to your staff using informal communication channels, especially during a change, you should stop immediately. Using this mode of communication to disseminate information to your staff, as opposed to a structured approach to communicating, is detrimental to your change efforts.

Van Vuuren and Elving (2008) argued that organizations should try and limit the amount of informal communication as much as possible since this can destroy or disturb all kinds of formal communication. However, in the absence of formal communication and information rumors and grapevine discussions are filling the gap. Many change efforts are poorly managed; simply because managers are of the opinion that withholding information ensures that people will learn what is happening only through official channels. But this has proven to be incredibly wrong, and as a result, the grapevine has always bloomed when this happens, according to Galpin. Therefore, formal communication activities were often supplemented and, in some cases, usurped by the grapevine.

However, many people have argued a totally different point of view. Sinetar for example, indicated that inflicting an aggressive, formal communication program upon an organization in an attempt to manage change will not succeed, yet this is what many companies ask their HR department to do. On the other hand, an informal communication forum can encourage brainstorming, active listening, and participative involvement, which can be a powerful tool for managing people and issues during a change process. Informal communication is 'concerned with the flow of information outside the authorized channels in the organization therefore, the importance of informal communication needs to be considered because it will help formal communication activities. Informal communication fills the information vacuum when formal communication fails to reduce the uncertainty and anxiety that typically accompanies organizational change but it must be controlled to prevent rumor-mongering. Regaining control of information amid rumors is extremely difficult. The longer a rumor is allowed, the more tedious it is to replace with valid information. Many people try to fight rumors with rumors; however, the only effective way to combat rumors is with facts. When many rumors exist, more facts must be communicated to combat the rumors.

In some organizations, management often neglects employees, and as a result, that informal communication channel (grapevine) spreads throughout all levels of the organization like a plague. Change, especially a transformational change, a merger or an acquisition, engenders fear in the hearts of many people. If the information is limited, it adds to the anxiety; worse yet, if rumors of layoff and relocation are circulating. In cases like these, management should do everything possible to eliminate these rumors with credible information that will allow employees to manage their fears and anxieties.

It is imperative.

Leaders choose to forget that change impacts people, and it is up to the leadership to provide some reassurance to their team with facts, not 'hearsay" or "what was heard by the side." It cannot work like that. Holly Green indicated in her article that employees who spend time trying to find out what is going on generally do not gain the best or most accurate information. Rapid, accurate communication is critical to younger employees who grew up with information at their fingertips. Accustomed to the instantaneous communication of the internet, they feel left out when managers fail to answer their questions, or get them up to speed on projects, changes, or organizational issues. Implementing significant change is complex and challenging. Change impacts people, and to successfully lead individuals during a change, leaders must be able to communicate effectively. Holly further indicated that poor communication is the best grapevine fertilizer.

When communicating with people consistently and frequently, they will not depend on the grapevine. However, if you leave your team in the dark on valuable information and individuals believe they can obtain fairly reliable facts from sources other than the formal communication channels, the grapevine will inevitably grow, derailing your whole change process. I am totally against using and even promoting the use of grapevine communication during any change; it often leads to a heightened level of resistance among employees. However, if the CEO or a manager uses informal conversations with their employees to reinforce what was communicated formally, it's not a problem. These interactions should be encouraged because it allows the leadership to communicate the message of the change consistently.

It is important to note that the information must be consistent with the formal communication from management. If the information lacks consistency, all aspects of the change will be broken down. Therefore, it makes absolutely no sense to emphasize consistency if the information is not valid and cannot be substantiated.

15
USING COMMUNICATION TO ERADICATE RESISTANCE

"When information about a change is inconsistent, people tend to resist it."

Resistance is inevitable; as a leader you cannot run from it or hide from it. Change always brings some element of fear for many people; the leadership job is to allay those fears and communicate the benefits of change, especially in the initial stages of the change. According to Dr. Cheng, organizational change often triggers intense emotions, sometimes leading to resistance. For example, loss or anticipated loss of control, routines, traditions, status, and relationships can lead to fear, frustration, anxiety, resentment, grief and depression.

Some have compared these emotions to the grieving process associated with major traumatic events such as death and dying. However, Eriksson argues that in environments of rapid and continuous change, these emotions can be exacerbated by an emotional residue of fatigue and lethargy left over from past change initiatives. Once the reality of the change starts to manifest itself, many people tend to react negatively, and as such, developing strategies to mitigate resistance is vital. The Change Curve model, describes the four stages most people go through as they adjust to change. It is imperative that leaders recognize these stages since they will significantly impact the outcome of the change, which can be used to determine where the resistance is located and what strategies can be employed to combat these resistors.

For example, an initial reaction to change may be shock or denial, as employees react to the challenges of the status quo. This first stage can particularly affect individuals who have not previously experienced major change. It is common for people to convince themselves that the change isn't actually going to happen, or if it does, it won't affect them. At this stage, communication is key. Reiterating what the actual change is, the effects it may have, and providing as much reassurance as possible, will all help to support individuals experiencing these feelings. Stage one is critical, and communication must be a priority.

For many organizations, this is the "danger zone," and if poorly managed, the organization may descend into crisis or chaos. Again, communication and support will play a vital role in minimizing and mitigating the problems that people will experience, for example.

- Explaining the why of the change.
- The selection of your communication channels.
- Tailoring your message to the different stakeholder groups.
- Maintaining consistency in your message and continuously repeating the message.
- Leadership commitment and the important role of the line manager.

Making sense? You see how everything comes together. Good change communications reduce anxiety by explaining what is not changing and how the organization will act to minimize the perceived downsides of the change. Change communications must withstand harsh scrutiny from the start to inspire genuine belief and confidence during the process. According to Kotter (1995), resistance should also be expected, but the management approach to this resistance will ultimately decide the employee's willingness to accept the change. Change is sometimes necessary and inevitable; unfortunately, employees sometimes view change as a direct attack on their performance or an unnecessary whim of management.

Change resistance is neither capricious nor mysterious, but in most cases, resistance arises from threats to traditional norms and ways of doing things. As a result, it is a fundamental tenet of human behavior to resist any change. Michael Armstrong (2007) argued that communication about a proposed change should be carefully prepared and worded so that unnecessary fears are allayed. It is interesting to note that Armstrong suggested that all available channels, for example, written documents, newsletters, and the intranet, should be used. However, face-to-face communication, direct from managers to individuals, or through a team briefing system is always best.

A critical success factor in mitigating resistance is the communication of the vision. Vision serves to inspire action, focus attention, and create a new social structure in the organization. Moreover, a vision that is understood is more likely to engender a favorable reaction to the change. John P. Kotter's 8-step change model also indicated that a strong vision would help determine the success of a change. According to Kotter, it is vital to communicate the vision frequently and powerfully, so it can act as a deterrent to resistance, but it is important to note that this communication needs to be consistent, frequent, and not a one-off meeting. The late Dr. Myles Munroe, famous pastor and inspirational speaker, indicated that "vision is the capacity to see further than your eyes can look." If management neglects or chooses to ignore communicating the vision to staff, chances are, the entire process will continue to experience problems, but more importantly, the company will forever be in a change mode with no clear sight of ever-changing.

Leaders must recognize that vision is a vital tool that inspires people to believe in the change, and as a result, leadership must first envision what the change will be and communicate that vision to their staff. It is the responsibility of management to give individuals, especially in the initial stages, the ability to see beyond their eyes in an attempt to mitigate resistance, but more importantly, to win the hearts and minds of staff and generate that positive excitement about the change.

As mentioned above, never believe that your staff has heard the communication too many times. You must endlessly repeat the message until it becomes a deeply seated aspect of your employee's daily habit. Be constant and consistent with your message and the vision of the change. To avoid resistance, change leaders should formulate a more structured approach to dialogue involving their employees.

Some of these are face-to-face communication, questionnaires, formal surveys, and focus groups as methods for coping with potential and actual resistance to change. Klein (1996) agrees and states that communication can be used to reduce resistance, minimize uncertainty, and improve commitment to the change process; this may, in turn, enhance motivation and retention among employees. The success stories of Ford, Starbucks, Xerox, and Apple can be attributed to the effective communication skills of their leaders throughout the transformation process. This was mainly due to the leaders' effective use of communication to drive their transformational process. However, achieving this was not an easy feat. Leading such a change required serious soul-searching, fortitude, and self-belief. As leaders, we must find inspiration within ourselves to keep the fire burning to help our team and our company reach their full potential.

PART 3

FINDING YOUR INSPIRATION

16

SOMETIMES WHEN THINGS ARE FALLING APART, THEY MAY ACTUALLY BE FALLING INTO PLACE

'Every time I thought I was being rejected from something good, I was actually being re-directed to something better.' - Steve Maraboli

When things in our life seem to go wrong, we often feel it's the end of the world because we can't see further than what's right in front of us. It's only when we look back after we've survived the storm do we realize that those "broken" parts are pieces that make up the beautiful picture that is our destiny. For example, when James's position at his organization became redundant due to an organizational-wide restructuring a couple of years ago, James was sad and depressed because he firmly believed it was the end of his life.

That experience almost broke him, but in many instances; for everything to come together, things need to fall apart first. Not getting what we want can be a huge step toward reaching a bigger dream, according to Rachel Brathen. To be persistent in the pursuit of your dreams, despite the challenges, despite the setbacks, requires you to have a strong will and a mind diabolically focused on your goals. When I listened to Chris Gardner's story and his unshakable faith and determination to become a stockbroker, I said to myself, "can I do that." The man slept in a subway station toilet with his toddler son. He enrolled in a training program that offered no salary. He didn't have enough money to raise the deposit to rent an apartment, bed down in parks, at church shelters, or under his desk at work after everyone else had gone home to pursue his dream of becoming a stockbroker. Through painstaking sacrifice and struggle, Mr. Gardner thrived in his job, and at the end of his training, he became a full-time employee and eventually a multimillionaire.

What are you willing to give up for your dream?

When you have that type of belief and you are prepared to go against popular opinion, believing in something so much you can feel it without touching it, you have now entered the world of faith. And even if it doesn't work out, that's all right. According to T.D. Jakes:

"If you are not sure about your life purpose, try something; even if the thing you are trying is not the thing, that's all right because that thing you are trying will lead you to the thing you are supposed to be doing."

I will not kid you; sometimes, the journey is challenging, and sometimes, you will doubt yourself. I can recall listening to Les Brown on running towards your dreams, and Les said he was sleeping and bathing in his office because he fell on some difficult times. Further, in his presentation, Les said, "I was sitting on the floor in the office watching out the window asking myself can I do this." It was hard, but he held on and made it at the end. You must always remember we are never rejected. There are no mistakes. No could haves. No should-haves. Everything that happens comes along because it simply needs to happen. You are a reflection of greatness; don't lose sight of that! There have been countless challenges that you thought were bigger than you, but you're still here every job you were denied for opened the door to new opportunities. Every relationship that hurt you led you to your true love.

Every mistake you thought would be the end pointed you toward an incredible success. In fact, according to Paul Hudson, you hear it all the time people hitting rock bottom before they bounce back up and soar. You must make room for the new by ridding yourself of the old. Unfortunately, when things do fall apart for a person, they break down in a rather devastating way. Staying positive when your world is crumbling around you is no easy task. Yet, in the end, you will see that every negative thing that happens is pushing you toward the next phase of growth in your life.

As JK Rollings puts it, rock bottom became the solid foundation on which I rebuilt my life. It is often a sign to turn your life around or go in a different direction, and in hindsight, you only become aware when the storm has passed. On your life journey, you will experience setbacks, failures, and rejection; How you react to these experiences, however, will determine if you grow from it or sulk in self-pity.

Obstacles and rejections are merely stepping-stones to something great, but you must change your attitude and not take rejection personally. Redirect your rejection and use it for something good; will it be easy at the time? Hell no, but in the end, it will be worth it. When you feel stuck and everything you are trying is not bearing any fruit, dig deep, bring forth your faith, and never give up. It will all be revealed in the end.

17

GREAT LEADERS ARE HUMBLE ENOUGH TO ADMIT THEIR MISTAKES AND LEARN FROM THEIR FAILURES

"As the leader, let your team know there's no shame in making mistakes and most importantly you have their backs when it happen."

"If we want to move forward and see Apple healthy and prospering again, we have to let go of this notion that for Apple to win, Microsoft has to lose. We have to embrace a notion that for Apple to win, Apple has to do a really good job...and if we screw up and we don't do a good job, it's not somebody else's fault, it's our fault. So, the era of competition between Apple and Microsoft is over as far as I'm concerned. This is about getting Apple healthy, this is about Apple being able to make incredibly great contributions to the industry and to prosper again."

--Steve Jobs, CEO, Apple Inc, at the 1997 Macworld Expo

As any great leader will tell you, they have made many mistakes along the way. They will admit that the collective insight from bad decisions taught them invaluable lessons and how to see opportunities in everything and anticipate the unexpected more quickly. Steve Jobs was very transparent about Apple's challenges at the 1997 Macworld Expo. Jobs knew that the only way Apple could become Apple again was to embrace the mistakes made, learn from what went wrong and create a culture that would allow everyone at Apple to produce insanely great products again. Jobs set the tone for everyone to follow when Apple got the 150 Million investment from Microsoft, which allowed the healing process to begin.

Leaders will make mistakes; there's no denying that fact, but what separates the greats from everyone else is that they have the fortitude to admit their wrongdoings so that those around them can also benefit from their learnings. They call this wisdom, and many leaders lack it because they are too proud to recognize mistakes as valuable learning moments for themselves and others. There are many so-called leaders who love to blame others when mistakes happen; have you ever experienced that? I have seen people in leadership positions duck and throw their people under the bus when mistakes happen, leading to mistrust, lack of inspiration, and the fear of trying anything new.

As a leader, you're responsible for everything in your organization, and you'll rightly be held accountable for everything that happens, good or bad. But that's the price of leadership; according to John Maxwell, if you want the perks of leadership, you must pay the price. So, this begs the question, what type of leader are you? Do you fail to take any responsibility for any errors that may happen in your department and, by extension, in your company; do your actions shift from doing the right thing to covering your behinds in many instances? Pointing fingers rather than accepting personal responsibility, hiding errors rather than fixing them, and allowing minor problems to become big ones because they're inadequately addressed. All leaders make regrettable decisions, and your team will make mistakes as well;

as a matter of fact, if you or your team have yet to make any bad decisions, they are not taking enough risks or learning enough to continue growing as a leader. Everyone makes mistakes; no one is perfect, but how you handle the aftermath of that mistake is the key. According to HS Burney, as a leader, you need to defend and advocate for your people. Don't publicly air their mistakes in front of others in the company. Even if the mistake is high-profile, think about absorbing the consequences yourself instead of shoving your team member in the line of fire.

When you lead people, you are now responsible for them; as Simon Sinek rightfully indicated, when you become a leader, you must transition from being responsible for the job to being responsible for the people who are responsible for the job, and that means taking responsibility for someone else's mistake. If you're in the driver's seat, it's your responsibility to bear the brunt of the blow, even if the person in the backseat caused the crash. This will engender loyalty with your team and provide some psychological safety for your team as well. When your team knows that their leader has their back, they will give their all to ensure their leader succeeds.

Great leaders ensure that poor choices don't compound their mistakes. They also make sure they learn from their mistakes and develop actions to handle the situation differently in the future. Remember that mistakes are vital to our growth; we often put way too much pressure on ourselves to seek some unrealistic ideal of perfection. The most extraordinary people in their felids have made countless mistakes; they didn't give up. Instead, they persevered and inspired many people to follow their example; as Albert Einstein puts it, a person who never made a mistake never tried anything new.

18

LEARNING AND GROWING FROM YOUR CHALLENGES

"If it doesn't challenge you, it won't change you."

Early in Denzel Washington's career, for example, he auditioned for a part in a Broadway musical; a perfect role for him, he thought, except for the fact that Denzel didn't get the job. But here's the thing about the story. He didn't quit; he didn't fall back. Instead, Denzel Washington walked out of there to prepare for the next audition, and the next audition, and the next audition. He prayed and prayed, but continued to fail, and fail, and fail, but it didn't matter because there's an old saying: "If you hang around a barbershop long enough, sooner or later you will get a haircut. You will catch a break."

In 2010 Denzel Washington starred in a play called Fences on Broadway, and he won a Tony Award for his outstanding performance; but here's the kicker, it was at that Court Theatre, the same theatre where Denzel Washington failed in his very first audition. So this begs the question. Do you have the guts to fail while you run after your dreams and goals, or are you living your life so cautiously that you are not even trying anything new, and if that's the case, you have already failed by default, according to JK Rowling. Sometimes challenges tend to make us grow as professionals and individuals, but the key is accepting the challenge, learning from it, and growing from it. The late Dr. Myles Munroe, a very inspirational and gifted speaker and pastor, said in one of his many lectures that true leaders love challenges. It helps them grow. Sometimes it may be difficult to understand the reason for the challenges, but in hindsight, you needed those lessons to help you make better decisions and choices.

It may come in many forms: someone betrayed your confidence, your project was delayed, your assignment was late, you failed an exam, your best friend was ill, you had a problem with your parents, or you broke up with your girlfriend or boyfriend. The list can go on and on, but if you look at each situation, there is something to learn from each scenario. As a matter of fact, because of that challenge, you are in a much better position now to make an intelligent decision and to conduct your due diligence to ensure that the situation never happens again, and if it does happen, you can make the right decision to mitigate the challenge.

To achieve the highest success, you must embrace the prospect of failure. Whether you are a renowned business owner, executive, politician, father, mother, writer, priest or pastor, I assure you no one is without mistakes. I am 100% sure they have failed countless times before, and like you, they are human; failure is part of the journey,' and no matter how much you try to avoid it, you cannot. So instead, you must learn how to handle it, embrace the lessons, get comfortable with it, and move on.

When James Quincey became the CEO of Coca-Cola, he called upon the rank-and-file managers to get beyond the fear of failure that dogged the company since the "New Coke" fiasco of so many years ago. Quincey said, "If we're not making mistakes, we're not trying hard enough." According to Pauline Estrem, when we take a closer look at the great thinkers throughout history, a willingness to take on failure isn't a new or extraordinary thought at all. From the likes of Augustine, Darwin, and Freud to today's business mavericks and sports legends, failure is as powerful a tool as any in reaching great success.

"Failure and defeat are life's greatest teachers [but] sadly, most people, and particularly conservative corporate cultures, don't want to go there," says Ralph Heath, managing partner of Synergy Leadership Group and author of Celebrating Failure: The Power of Taking Risks, Making Mistakes and Thinking Big. "Instead, they choose to play it safe, to fly under the radar, repeating the same safe choices over and over again. They operate under the belief that if they make no waves, they attract no attention; no one will yell at them for failing because they never attempt anything great at which they could fail (or succeed)."

Some people get paralyzed by failure, and they believe if they fail at something, that's it; "my life is over." But the sweetest victory is the most difficult one. The one that requires you to reach down deep inside, to fight with everything you've got, to be willing to leave everything out there on the battlefield—without knowing, until that do-or-die moment, burning all your boats with no safety net of retreat.

Develop A New Mindset

You must develop a mindset of success and overcome many obstacles on your journey to success. You can ask any successful entrepreneur, sportsperson, writer, or anybody who has experienced some success; you have to focus your mind on your vision, see it as having already been achieved, believe in your heart you will achieve it and work extremely hard to get it. There are no shortcuts. But it all starts with changing your mindset and embracing failure as part of the journey.

You cannot run away from it. I have failed at many things in my short time on this earth. I can remember that feeling—that feeling of despair, the lack of self-confidence and no motivation to try again. Yup, I have been there. To some people failing at anything feels like giving a piece of your life away. No one likes to fail, but sometimes failures do occur, and in many instances, it comes to help us find the courage or to prepare us for something great.

So many people fall into the trap of talking about their past mistakes repeatedly, but it makes no sense talking about your past. Don't torture yourself on what could have been; you must put that behind you. It will drag you down if you don't, but it all starts with your mindset and embracing life's challenges. Success does not happen overnight. You may sometimes feel lost while finding it difficult to get out of bed. It will not be easy, but guess what?

You are strong enough to overcome all the adversity in your life. You must decide to live life on a new level, and according to Les Brown, you can either live your dreams or live your fears. So don't be afraid to try new things; don't allow fear to paralyze you. I listened to a sermon from TD Jakes about a person trapped on the top floor of a burning eight stories building. The fire is blazing throughout the whole building, and the only route to escape from the inferno is a window. When the Firefighters arrive at the building, the person can jump to the ground onto the Firefighters' net but is afraid. You see, the person is afraid of the solution and is also scared of the problem, and as a result, when situations like this occur, people prefer to stay right there without moving. You may be in that position. You know the problem but afraid of the solution. Deep down in your heart, you can achieve so much more in life, but you are scared to make the change. To achieve your personal best, to reach unparalleled heights, to make the impossible possible, you can't fear failure, you must think big, and you must get comfortable with being uncomfortable.

Sometimes we're so focused on not failing that we don't aim for success at all, instead settling for a life of mediocrity while complaining and blaming everyone and everything for the stagnation in our lives. If you want to be great and experience the heights of success like the greats in leadership or any other profession, you must get comfortable with failure, and you must explore life outside your comfort zone. God created you for a reason, and the circumstances may bring you closer to your purpose in life.

Remember, if you find your purpose, you will find your passion, and challenges sometimes push us in the right direction. You must develop a mindset that when the challenge comes, face it head-on. Don't retreat to your comfort zone; you may be holding yourself back from something great. Failures may come, but you must learn from them and turn them into positive outcomes. Life is never easy, and it can beat down on you like a ton of bricks. However, you must have that self-belief.

You must believe that everything will work out despite the setbacks. Once you develop a mindset of success and do not allow fear to hold you back, you will start to experience a revolutionary change in your life. Failure helped with the development of my mental toughness, and if I did not have those moments of crisis in my life, I am 100% certain, with all the responsibilities I have now and the demands placed on my life, it would be extremely difficult to navigate any troubled waters. You may be tempted to ask, "why is this happening to me" just like I did but take solace from the fact that you can learn from these experiences and one good day benefit from it.

Leaders are called upon to make countless decisions, and sometimes things inevitably go wrong. Many leaders may see admitting a mistake as a sign of weakness, but the opposite is true in many instances. Accepting and acknowledging your errors has the potential to strengthen your relationships with your team. Admitting your mistakes communicates in a powerful way that you believe in the relationships you've developed. People around you need to know that you are human. They need to know you have the trust in them and in your own leadership to say, "I'm sorry. I didn't handle XYZ well. I take full responsibility. Here's what we need to do to get things right and back on track…."

The time has come to view every mistake as an opportunity rather than a weakness, according to Steve Adubato, Ph.D. This change in outlook will stimulate personal growth, strengthen relationships, and enhance efficiency and effectiveness. The truth is that there shouldn't be shame in making a mistake. How will you learn? How will you grow if you are so afraid to try something new? Chances are it may not work out, but that's life; there's no disgrace in that; the disgrace should be in failing to admit, correct, and learn from it. The sign of a superior leader is not that they avoid making mistakes or running away from their challenges; it's that when they do happen, they are humble enough to admit it and learn from them while never giving up on their dream.

19

STRATEGIES TO HELP YOU DEAL WITH A PERSONAL CRISIS AT WORK

'Rock bottom became the solid foundation on which I rebuilt my life.' - J.K. Rowling

How do you deal with a personal crisis and work at the same time? A friend of mine was going through a significant dilemma in her personal life to the point where the walls around her were closing down on her with no means of escape. With tears running down her face, she asked me, how do you deal with it? How do you deal with it? My friend separated from her husband because of the constant abuse, and with nowhere to go, she slept in her car with her baby for two nights. But to compound the situation further, she still had to report to work, and knowing the person, she was ashamed to tell anyone at work what was going on with her personal life.

Hell, I didn't even know.

But how do you deal with a crisis like that and still function at work without completely losing it? Deborah Shane, a career author, featured writer, speaker, and media and marketing consultant, says it's impossible to completely separate your personal and work life. Therefore, it is difficult to evade your crisis at work, but she warns, "Don't be a drama queen or a toxic person." Jacquelyn Smith wrote a great article about how you deal with a personal crisis at work, and I want to share with you some of the strategies Smith outlined in the article. The strategies are constructive and straightforward, and they can help to bring some stability to your life if you are dealing with anything similar to what my friend was dealing with.

Tell Your Employer

For some people, this will sound crazy, "tell my manager, he/she will never understand." Nancy Collamer, a career coach at MyLifestyleCareer.com, says it depends on the crisis. In the case of a sudden, severe, and dramatic crisis, you should definitely tell your employer, she says. "People tend to be highly sympathetic in these types of situations and are often eager to help. Don't shut them out."

"Most crisis take up time and energy, and therefore will have an impact on your work," Terry says. "Whenever you anticipate your work being affected, you need to inform your employer." The question of whether or not to tell your employer in other types of crisis situations is a bit more difficult to answer. A couple of questions to consider: Is your employer supportive and someone who you can trust?

Is this a situation you feel comfortable discussing? Can you realistically handle this situation during non-work hours? If you are at a crisis level and it is affecting your work, you have no choice but if it's something you can handle and you don't feel comfortable talking about your issues with your employer, don't share; deal with it.

Don't Share Too Much or Too Little

If you do decide to share, or if the problem is so disruptive that there is simply no choice but to share, choose your words carefully, Collamer says. "Explain the situation clearly without going overboard on the details--particularly when describing situations that might leave the other party feeling uneasy." There is a fine line between providing not enough and too much information. "You don't want to be a soap opera, but you don't want to be so private that people don't have the opportunity to support you," says Melissa Hopp, vice president of administrative services at the Community College of Baltimore County, Maryland.

Tell Co-workers On A Need-to-know Basis

Everyone affected by your performance needs to understand, but they don't need every detail, Mistal says. Think about the people you work with and how any changes in your work or schedule, as a result of the crisis, will affect them. "I would only tell co-workers who you know well, and you have that kind of trusting relationship with," Shane adds. "Having a small support team at work is very helpful during crisis times." But she says to take extreme caution, as co-workers may betray your confidence. Having your personal business aired around the office will add unnecessary stress.

Stay Positive and Keep Your Emotions In Check

"Keep your poise and positive attitude and act as best you can daily," Shane says. Try to keep your emotions under control, Collamer adds. "If possible, wait to speak with your employer until you've had a chance to settle your nerves and reflect on the situation. The last thing you want to do is dissolve into a puddle of tears in your boss's office. It can be helpful to rehearse the conversation ahead of time with a trusted friend." Another way to stay positive at work: surround yourself with positive co-workers. "Limit the time you spend with negative people," Stearns says. "Maximize your time with hopeful, positive, kind, empathetic, unselfish people who care about you and live their own lives optimistically.

Say, Thank You

Once the crisis passes, don't forget to express your gratitude, Collamer says. It doesn't have to be a grand gesture; something as simple as writing a thank you note can be a very powerful gesture.

Dealing with any crisis will have its stressful moments, and if you are lucky enough to work in a very supportive environment, hats off to you; at least you can get some support from your employer. Unfortunately, not all organizations are made equal, and in these types of companies, a personal crisis means nothing to a company that shows no care for their employees. When Sheryl Sandberg's husband died unexpectedly in Mexico, she struggled to recover her footing at home and work. Sandberg began to write about her pain and authored a long essay about her suffering and sense of isolation and posted it on Facebook, where she serves as Chief Operating Officer (and has nearly 2 million followers).

The piece started a global conversation about how people can cope with a tragedy. From that experience, Sheryl learned that "It's important for all our companies to give everyone the time off they need to grieve and heal. And once people come back to work, it's important to help them realize that they can still contribute and not to write them off because they're sick or grieving." My friend, thank God, got some help and worked through the situation, it is not 100% perfect, but she is coping well and adjusting. I don't know the extent of her employer involvement, but she got some support at work. But you know what? Life will always pitch you a curveball along the way. You don't know what hand you will be dealt, but if you are at a point where the situation is too much for you to handle, seek help, seek genuine people who want to help, pray, never doubt yourself, keep the faith and believe with all your heart that everything will work out.

20

FIND YOUR WORK, NEVER SETTLE FOR A JOB

"Life has so much meaning, but you need to find your work to live a rewarding life."

Do you often struggle with feelings of anxiety, sadness, or stress at the start of a new workweek? Do you find yourself lacking motivation and enthusiasm for your job?

In today's fast-paced and competitive world, finding meaningful work that aligns with your passions, values, and ambitions is crucial. While a job may provide financial stability, settling for just any job can lead to dissatisfaction and a lack of fulfillment in the long run. Instead, it is important to embark on a journey of self-discovery and actively seek out work that brings joy, purpose, and a sense of personal growth.

Many people accidentally "fall" into a career they dislike, and often due to their financial situations, they remain at a job that offers nothing but despair and heartache. Interestingly, a recent survey found that over 80% of workers are disengaged from their careers. The average person spends a third of their life at work, and to spend that amount of time in a job you do not like can be very disheartening. Some people strive for success at work and pour 100% of themselves into their careers, but somewhere along the way, that emotional feeling slowly fades away, leaving them feeling stuck, trapped, bored, frustrated, drained, duped, or depressed. I know this feeling because I've also experienced all these feelings at times in my career. Many people go through life without finding their work and settling for a job. Now you may be wondering what's the difference. Your job is what your employer pays you to do; your work is what you were born to do.

If you find yourself aimlessly thinking as I have done before, "Why am I still at this job" you have settled for a paycheck and still looking for your work. According to the late Dr. Munroe, some people go through life frustrated, finding it difficult to get up on Monday morning, go to a job they hate, get stuck in traffic. Doing this all their life without knowing the real joys of life.

Life has so much meaning, but you need to find your work to live a rewarding life. You need to find that thing that gives you the confidence to get up the next day. You need to find that thing that brings a smile to your face every day of the week. That thing that makes you look forward to Monday morning. Some people have found their work, but I must tell you, many people are still looking for their purpose in life.

Once you find your area of gifting, you will never settle for a job in your life again. I have been in several positions, and I can tell you, on every single one, I always asked myself why I was there; I was very irritable and never focused on my task. So you know what? I left one job after the next, hoping the next one would be the correct fit. I never found it. I blame everything and everyone without looking within and genuinely asking myself what I want to do with my life. I read a very informative article from Deepak Chopra about his trip to India and the best advice he ever got.

"Match your job, your career, and your calling."

If you found your work but stuck in a job far different from your purpose in life, you will never be satisfied. As a matter of fact, you will be withholding something our generation and the generations to come are supposed to receive from you. It is imperative to make every effort to find your purpose, find your work; if you haven't found it yet, keep looking, don't give up.

Steps to Finding Your Work

a. Self-reflection: Take the time to understand your passions, values, and strengths. Consider what brings you joy, what makes you feel fulfilled, and what kind of impact you want to make in the world.

b. Explore your options: Research various industries, career paths, and opportunities that align with your interests. Attend workshops, seminars, and networking events to gain insights and make connections.

c. Experiment and iterate: Don't be afraid to try new things and step outside your comfort zone. Seek internships, volunteer work, or part-time roles to gain practical experience and discover what resonates with you.

d. Continuous learning: Invest in your personal and professional development. Take courses, attend workshops, and read books to enhance your skills and broaden your knowledge base.

e. Seek mentorship and guidance: Surround yourself with mentors and individuals who can offer advice and support. Their insights and experiences can provide valuable perspectives on your journey.

As I mention before and its worth mentioning again from T.D Jakes, if you try something and it doesn't work out, that's OK; keep trying it will be the thing that leads you to the thing you are purpose to do. Everything in life is connected; every experience is a preparation for the thing you were destined to become. Don't be afraid to try something new; even if it doesn't work out, that's OK; those experiences will bring you closer to your purpose.

Steve Jobs said something very telling:

"Your work is going to fill a large part of your life, and the only way to be truly satisfied is to do what you believe is great work. And the only way to do great work is to love what you do. If you haven't found it yet, keep looking. Don't settle. As with all matters of the heart, you'll know when you find it. And, like any great relationship, it just gets better and better as the years roll on. So keep looking until you find it. Don't settle".

To make sense of your life, you must find your calling (purpose), which should fit your job and career. Settling for a job that does not fulfill you on a deeper level can lead to long-term dissatisfaction and a lack of purpose. Instead, invest time and effort into finding your work – a vocation that aligns with your passions, values, and ambitions. If you don't, it will always be a struggle to get yourself out of bed every morning, and life is too short to waste it away at a job that does nothing to help you become the very best version of yourself.

Instead, embrace the journey of self-discovery, overcome challenges with resilience, and make a positive impact on the world. Remember, life is too short to settle for anything less than work that truly brings you joy, fulfillment, and a sense of purpose.

CONCLUSION

When you are called to lead, you are called to serve, and you must be willing to place the needs of others above your own. When you are called a leader, you must inspire and motivate your team daily to make a difference. That's what we call leadership, and that's what real leaders do. Many leaders forget that leading others should be revered more than anything else. Being the leader means that you have been placed in a position to serve others.

Some individuals in leadership roles tend to sidestep responsibility, deflect criticism onto their team members, misuse their authority and put their own interests ahead of their team when confronted with challenges. Nevertheless, it is important to note that effective leadership requires a different approach altogether. You are privileged to be in a position where you can direct, shape, and focus people's potential toward a specific result. When you are given the responsibility to lead, you are given a tremendous opportunity to influence many people's lives positively, a responsibility you should never take for granted. Everyone has the potential to lead, but unfortunately, everyone doesn't want to pay the price for leadership. No one said leadership was easy, and it's definitely not for the faint of heart. Becoming one of the greats of leadership requires making some very tough and unpopular decisions. Accepting responsibility when things go wrong while giving away the credit when things go well; running headfirst in the fire when everyone else is running in the next direction. Leadership will have its challenging days, but the satisfaction of knowing that you are impacting and making a difference every day far outweighs any challenge on any given day. Leadership requires work and continual self-development to ensure that your leadership is equipped to deal with the dynamic pace of change in our world today.

As leaders, we have a lot of demands placed on our time, and as such, we must make that time for ourselves and ensure that our life is full of joy and happiness. Although our work drives us, we also need some balance in our lives as well. Mindfulness practices like meditation and self-reflection can help leaders connect with their inner selves. By cultivating self-awareness and practicing self-care, leaders can replenish their energy, reduce stress, and tap into their inner wisdom and inspiration.

Celebrating milestones and successes along your leadership journey is crucial. Acknowledging achievements and practicing gratitude for big and small things in your help reinforces a sense of accomplishment and motivation. Celebrations also help leaders appreciate their progress and recharge their inspiration for future endeavors. By accessing our inner inspiration, we can unleash our full potential to cope with any daily challenges that come our way. Let's embrace this power that resides within us all and use it to positively impact the world.

ABOUT GIFFORD THOMAS

I am the founder of Leadership First and the author of the Amazon Best Seller, The Inspirational Leader, Inspire Your Team To Believe In The Impossible. I have over 15 years of experience in leadership development and I am passionate about empowering leaders to create excellent organizations that inspire and motivate people to achieve their full potential.

Leadership First is a platform that reaches over 5.3M+ leaders every day with the best inspirational leadership quotes and articles from the best leadership minds in the world. I am also a member of the Harvard Business Review Advisory Council, a council member with GLG, an advisor with visasQ Inc, and one of the leading writers on Quora for Leadership Development. I am dedicated to assisting leaders navigate the disruptions and challenges of today's highly competitive world. My aim is to foster a culture of inspirational leadership that encourages all leaders to become the very best version of themselves.

THE INSPIRATIONAL LEADER, INSPIRE YOUR TEAM TO BELIEVE IN THE IMPOSSIBLE

Can you inspire your team's hearts and minds every day? If you can, your organization will become one of the best in the world, and your team will perform at heights you never imagine. The Inspirational Leader, Inspire Your

Team To Believe In The Impossible was written to help all leaders successfully navigate all the disruptions in today's fiercely competitive world; we need a new generation of leaders who care deeply for the well-being of their team and who understand that their people are the heart of their leadership. Whether you are the leader of a large, medium or small organization; a Teacher, a V.P., CEO, Father, Mother, Police Officer, or Hustler; this book was written to help you inspire your team to believe in the impossible.

REFERENCES

- Armstrong, M. (2007). *" the process of performance management". A handbook of human resource management practice.* 10th edition Kogan page Limited. UK pp 131

- Allen, R.S., Dawson, G.A., Wheatley, K.K., and White, C.S. (2004), 'Diversity Practices: Learning

- Brooks, K., Callicoat, J. & Siegerdt, G. (1979) The ICA communication audit and perceived communication effectiveness changes in 16 Audited organizations. *Human Communication Research*, 5 (2), p.130---137

- Balogun, J & Hope Hailey, V (2004) *Exploring Strategic Change*, 2nd ed. Prentice Hall/Financial Times

- Balogun, J & Hailey, H V (1999) *Exploring Strategic Change: designing the transition: levers and mechanisms.* Pearson Education Limited. England

- Brimm H and Murdock A (1998) Delivering the message in challenging times: the relative effectiveness of different forms of communicating change to a dispersed and part-time workforce, Total Quality Management, Vol.9, No.2/3, pp.167-180

- Berger, C. R., & Calabrese, R. J. (1975). Some explorations in initial interaction and beyond: Toward a development theory of interpersonal communication. *Human Communication Research, 1*, 99-112.

- Dess, G. et al., 1998. Transformational leadership: lessons from US experience. *Long Lange Planning*, 31 (5), pp.722-31.

- Ford, J. D., Ford, L. W., & McNamara, R. 2002. Resistance and the background conversations of change. *Journal of Organizational Change Management,* 15(1): 105–121.

- Goshal, S. and Bartlet, C., 1996. Rebuilding behavioural context: a blueprint for corporate renewal. *Sloan Management Review*, 37 (2), pp.23-26.

- Gioia, D.A. and Sims, H.P. (1986), "Cognitive-behavior connections: attribution and verbal behavior in leader-subordinate interactions",

- Hiatt (2006) How to implement successful change in our personal lives and professional careers: Building Awareness. United States.

- Maurer, R. (1997) transforming resistance HR focus vol 74 NO 10

- O'Connor, V. (1990), "Building internal communications (two-way) management-employee communications",

- Oshal, S. and Bartlett, C., 1995. Changing the role of top management: beyond structure to processes. *Harvard Business Review,* 73(1), pp.79-88.

- Price, A.D.F & Chahal, K. (2006). A strategic framework for change management. *Loughborough University-Construction Management and Economics,* 24, 237–251.

- Roberts and O'Reilly (1974) measuring organizational communication. Journal of applied psychology.

- Responses for Modern Organizations,'Development and Learning in Organizations, 18, 6, 13 – 15.

- Schein, E. (1992). Organizational culture and leadership (2nd ed.). San Francisco: Jossey-Bass.

- Senge, P., 2006. *The fifth discipline: the art and practice of the learning organization.* 2nd ed. New York: Doubleday.

- Stacks, D. and Salwen, M., 2009. *An Integrated approach to communication theory and research*. 2nd ed. Routledege: Oxon.

Online Resources

- Frahm J and Brown K., 2007. First steps: linking change communication to change receptivity [e-journal] 20 (3) Available through: Emerald Group Publishing Limited [Accessed 11 July 2011].

- Galpin, T., 2005. Pruning the grapevine [e-journal] 49 (4) Available through: ProQuest- ABI/Inform global &UK Newsstand. [Accessed 22 August 2011]

- Insead faculty and research working paper, 2008. The proof is in the pudding: an integrated, psychodynamic approach to evaluating a leadership development programme. Available at: http://ketsdevries.com/author/papers/PDF/Proof_in_the_Pudding_Evaluating_LD_programs_WP.pdf [Accessed 16 march 2011]

- Kotter, J., 1995. Leading Change: why transformational efforts fail. *Harvard Business Review*, [e-journal] 73 (2), pp.59-67. Available through: Business Source Complete [Accessed 17 February 2011].

- Van Vuuren, M. & Elving, W. J. L. (2008). Communication, sensemaking and change as a chord of three strands: practical implications and a research agenda for communicating organizational change", *Corporate Communications*, 13(3), 349-359. Available through: Emerald Group Publishing Limited. [Accessed 8

July 2011].

- Cheng, L. (2015). Enablers That Positively Impact Implementation of Organizational Change, [e-journal] 4(1), pp. 8. Available Through: GSTF Journal on Business Review (GBR) [Assessed 23 February 2018]

- Beatty, C. A (2015). Communicating During an Organizational Change, pp. 8-11. Available through: Queen's University IRC. [Assessed 20 February 2018]

Printed in Great Britain
by Amazon